THROUGH A LENS DARKLY

Through a Lens Darkly

Tracing Redemption in Film

Marjorie Hewitt Suchocki

CASCADE *Books* • Eugene, Oregon

Cascade Books
An Imprint of Wipf and Stock Publishers
199 W. 8th Ave., Suite 3
Eugene, OR 97401

www.wipfandstock.com

ISBN: 978-1-4982-0313-5

Cataloging-in Publication data:

Suchocki, Marjorie.

Through a lens darkly : tracing redemption in film / Marjorie Hewitt Suchocki.

p.; cm. Includes filmography.

ISBN: 978-1-4982-0313-5

1. Motion pictures—Religious aspects—Christianity. 2. Motion pictures—Religious aspects. 3. Christianity and culture. 4. Redemption. I. Title.

PN1995.9 R4 S93 2015

Manufactured in the U.S.A.

Paul and Lil

Contents

PROLOGUE

Through a Lens Darkly

Tracing Redemption in Film

What if we looked at a series of films by the same director and asked the question, how does this director resolve the problems set up for these characters? Would we find some continuity in the way each director defines and/or resolves the problems in successive films? Or does the director use different answers for similar problems? Such an investigation could be stimulating for any person who cares about film, but it would be especially rewarding for those film lovers who are also deeply interested in questions posed by religion or theology. There is a freshness to the issues we usually consider when they are taken up by those outside our normal fields of inquiry, and we are instructed by insights not our own.

Through a Lens Darkly takes up the challenge, with a caveat. This study is necessarily limited to a certain period of time in each director's career—but happily, the careers are ongoing, and more films are produced. Thus each chapter in this study must be open-ended enough for the discussion to be continued as further films enter the fray. In a sense this enriches the value of the current study, allowing the readers to follow the continuing twists and turns developed by each director. Woody Allen, for example, develops intriguing resolutions to his perennial problems of meaning, morality, and mortality in the two films I chose to conclude my seven-film study of his work—but the very next film he produced, after my chapter was completed, was *Blue Jasmine,* in which he rejects his resolutions and goes back to the insolubility of the problems!

I have chosen seven directors for this study, five of whom have written their own screenplays. Clint Eastwood and Ang Lee are the two directors who chose to work with screenplays written by others; Woody Allen, Joel and Ethan Coen, John Sayles, and Spike Lee write their own material. When the Coen brothers base their films on novels written by others, they themselves write the screenplays, choosing and changing the emphasis to suit their own creative genius. I am using but one film by my seventh director, Terrence Malick: the magnificent *Tree of Life.* While he has written and directed other films, in this one he explicitly addresses religious and theological problems, thus making it particularly pertinent as a coda to my study of films by the other six directors.

The subtitle of this work, *Tracing Redemption in Film*, betrays my theological interests. Much of my previous work has dealt with the traditional problems of sin, evil, and redemption as these have been addressed historically, and as they are currently addressed in process theology. The discipline of theology provides the parameters within which theologians work, and at the same time implicitly governs our forms of resolution. But our questions go beyond any discipline; they are the questions raised by life itself. What do the resolutions look like when they emerge outside of religious or theological inquiry? And so as a theologian I turn to the art of filmmaking, tracing resolutions—what theologians call redemption—as developed by seven superb masters of the craft.

Join me in the adventure—and take it beyond the confines of this book as you continue to follow these directors in their ongoing exploration of human existence through the art of film.

Good cinema *and* good theology to you!
Marjorie Hewitt Suchocki

Acknowledgments

MY DEEPEST THANKS TO friends and colleagues who gave constant encouragement for this book, particularly Kathy Black (Claremont School of Theology), Mary Elizabeth Moore (Boston University School of Theology), and Douglas Todd (journalist for the *Vancouver Sun*). I am particularly grateful to Doug for his valuable critical feedback on drafts of this manuscript. Deep thanks go as well to Jeanyne Slettom, whose creative mind gave me the title, *Through a Lens Darkly.*

1

Clint Eastwood

Violence and Resolution

Unforgiven (1992)
Mystic River (2002)
Million Dollar Baby (2004)
Gran Torino (2009)
Hereafter (2010)

THE THEOLOGICAL CHALLENGE IN the films of Clint Eastwood signals an apparent shift in Eastwood's response to the problem of violence. Within a twenty-year period, five of his films address resolutions to the issue. In the first two—the 1992 *Unforgiven* and the 2002 *Mystic River*—violence is repudiated as a response to violence. But in the next two films we consider, *Million Dollar Baby* (2004) and *Gran Turino* (2009), a very different resolution to violence is suggested—that of self-sacrificial love, where death is both accepted and given for the sake of the loved one. Death for the sake of saving another is itself a violent response to violence, and by exploring the implications of self-sacrificial love, Eastwood, unlike the other directors considered in this study, turns to an explicitly

Christian motif. Is that turn a contradiction to Eastwood's earlier two films, which eschew violent responses?

Violence

Both *Unforgiven* and *Mystic River* involve the question of crime and its just punishment. *Unforgiven* is an antiwestern western that gives us a caustic view of the romanticization of raw violence that usually occurs in westerns. A cowboy has taken his knife to a prostitute's face, angrily cutting her for what he takes as her disrespect. The other prostitutes in the brothel are rightly furious at this act, and the sheriff comes. He deems a bull whipping sufficient punishment for the crime, but the brothel's owner strongly objects: he has paid good money to ship that woman to his brothel, and he needs recompense for the damage to his property. And so instead of bullwhipping the cowboy and his companion, the sheriff allows them to go free, but they must pay the brothel owner six horses in recompense for the property damage. The women hear themselves reduced to mere property and gain no redress for their own suffering. There is no justice for them. Outraged, they pool their savings and offer a one-thousand-dollar bounty to anyone who will kill the offending cowboy.

This is the background that brings our two heroes, Bill Munny and Ned Logan, out of retirement. Both are former desperadoes who in middle age have settled into more traditional roles. Munny is now a widower, raising two children. But times are hard, and his farm is failing; his children are in need, and the one-thousand-dollar bounty is sufficient to persuade Munny this one last time that he should make his way via his gun. Logan joins him, not out of desire for a share of the money; he would far rather stay home. But he will not let his old friend go into danger without being at his side, helping him. And so Logan joins Munny as together they partner with the smart-alecky youth who tempted Munny with the bounty money in the first place. This young man idolizes these men of the old west, and longs to be the desperado he fancies them still to be. However, the older men are no longer killers; time and the love of their respective wives have tempered them. So we begin the story with point and counterpoint: the wannabe kid who can hardly wait to engage in violence, and the been-there-done-that older men whose distaste for violence is tempered only by their respective needs.

If these characters represent a past and future relation to violence, the tale unfolds by taking us back into the town and its present embroilment in violence, particularly embodied in its sheriff. The sheriff uses violence to repress violence. Backed up by his badge, he rules the town with his whip and his gun, imposing his own form of order. An interesting metaphor interrupts the film in the form of the house that the sheriff is building outside the town. Without architect or builder, he is attempting to build a home for himself. Just as the sheriff imposes his will on the town, so he also imposes his will upon the raw materials for his house—but he has no knowledge of what the materials can or can't do, and no knowledge of how things actually work together to create a home. The house provides a bit of comic relief in the film, but more deeply, it symbolizes an attempt to create a societal home simply through raw power, without adequate knowledge of the factors needed to create a viable society. More than raw power is needed.

And so the sheriff's reign over the town, while superficially effective, lacks the grounding in the common good that makes a community work in the first place. Into this situation ride our trio. Predictably, they run into trouble with the sheriff, mayhem ensues, but Munny devises a plan whereby he can kill the cowboy and earn the bounty. Logan, sickened by the violence, tries unsuccessfully to persuade Munny to desist. He has no heart for killing, not even to help out his friend. And so he bows out, leaving the two to their work as he himself mounts his horse and heads back home. Munny stays. When he and the youngster kill the cowboy, it is not in some dramatic shoot-out as the kid has envisioned, but in cold blood, as the cowboy is leaving his outhouse and heading back to the kitchen. There is no glory in the killing, and the kid vomits out his disgust. But nonetheless, he and Munny leave town with the one thousand dollars successfully pocketed. The youngster, however, has come face-to-face with the reality of taking human life as opposed to the fantasy of taking human life. Meanwhile, the sheriff has gathered together a posse to catch the men—but he only catches Logan, whom he brings back to the town, publicly tortures, and kills. Word comes to Munny about what has happened to his friend.

His old desperado persona returns: he goes back to the town enraged, and a western shoot-em-up follows as he proceeds to shoot the sheriff and four others in classic Clint Eastwood style. The closing scenes of the film show Munny's now-deserted farm, with the printed citation that our erstwhile hero has packed up his home and children and moved away from the wild west to the booming coast town of San Francisco.

The film suggests that while violence might establish a town, it cannot maintain the town. But there is no real resolution to violence in the film. Rather, the film argues that violence as an answer to violence yields only further violence, and that the taking of human life is not the answer to the evils we experience or cause. There is, however, an implied resolution, and this is given in the title itself. The film shows the circles of violence and despair that result through the impulse to get even, and therefore it shows the consequences of a failure to forgive. The film as a whole portrays the consequences of being unforgiving and unforgiven. Is forgiveness, then, the answer to violence? And what can forgiveness mean in the midst of such violence done to body and spirit? The film does not tell us what forgiveness is, only what ensues when forgiveness is lacking. As such, the film certainly incites curiosity as to the nature of this elusive virtue of forgiveness. If its lack can create such terrible mayhem, then forgiveness itself must be a stronger power than the mayhem it overcomes. But what, exactly, is forgiveness?

In many respects, *Mystic River* parallels *Unforgiven*, since this film also condemns vigilante justice as the answer to violence. *Mystic River*, like *Unforgiven*, pits vigilante justice against legal justice. Satisfactory legal justice is lacking in the earlier film, but it is strongly present in the later movie. *Mystic River* sets its stage with two crimes: a flashback to child molestation in the early 1970s, and a contemporary murder; both crimes frame the beginning of the film. As the eleven-year-old boy is abducted by a man posing as a law officer, we see the utterly poignant scene of the boy through the rear window of the car as he looks back at his two friends, left on the street behind. We are briefly shown the boy in a cellar begging not to be hurt again, and then we catch glimpses of his escape as he runs through the surrounding woods. The film then catapults us to the present-day events that quickly lead to murder, setting up the dynamics of violence calling for response.

The three boys of the beginning are now three men—acquaintances rather than friends. One is Jimmy, the father of the murdered girl. He lives on the edge of the law; in his youth he had served two years' time for robbery, but now he is supposedly straight. Another is Sean, the detective assigned to the murder case. And the third is Dave, the now-adult molested boy, who still suffers from the psychic damage inflicted through that original crime.

One issue raised by both *Unforgiven* and *Mystic River* is whether or not vigilante justice can in fact be just. In both films the answer is clearly no. Vigilante justice deems one punishment to be suitable for crime—and that is capital punishment, death. In *Unforgivien*, the prostitutes will not accept their demeaning, they will not accept offers of redress from one of the cowboys—for them nothing but death can atone for the crimes against them. And Jimmy, father of the murdered girl in *Mystic River*, likewise sees death as the answer to injury done to him, whether personally or through his family. In *Unforgiven*, the consequences of vigilante justice are physical and psychic mayhem, with the emphasis on the physical carnage. *Mystic River* explores the psychic consequences of vigilante justice. In the first film, there seems no justice available other than vigilante justice, for the legal system of the town is corrupt; whereas in the second film, the legal system operates—it just operates slowly, with careful checks and balances. Furthermore, the justice of the legal system robs the vigilante of the perverse pleasure of personal retaliation. In both films, vigilante justice reduces the sentence to only one: death. There are no nuances to be considered, no ambiguities clouding the issue. Absolute clarity is presupposed, and in the clarity of this judgment, death is the deserved punishment for grievance.

Even as both films depict this, they judge vigilante justice as wanting: vengeance is not a prerogative of the injured party, nor is death the single answer to all grievance. This is particularly interesting to those in the Christian tradition, for in important ways Christianity has also held that ultimately there is but one suitable punishment for any infraction of divine law, and that punishment is death. No mitigating factors are allowed: any sin at all, whether intentional or not, deserves both temporal and eternal death. Eastwood's later films will allow us to return to this issue. In *Unforgiven*, however, we have seen Logan refusing such so-called justice. The wisdom he has garnered leads him to walk away—but he is ensnared nonetheless, captured and reduced to worthlessness by the sheriff, who tortures and kills him. Munny likewise leaves his final mayhem dispirited; he goes back to his children and takes them away from the wild west—if indeed San Francisco in the 1880s qualifies as *away*. And the young would-be killer is sickened by the actuality of killing as opposed to his fantasies, and so in remorse he vows never to kill again. *Unforgiven*, far from vaunting vigilante justice, exposes its inhumaneness, its soul-destroying as well as body-destroying power. There is no forgiveness in such justice.

Mystic River, likewise, views vigilante justice with a sort of infinite sadness. The image of Dave as a doomed eleven-year-old in a car, looking back at his friends as he is driven to his place of abuse and spiritual death, is matched by the image of the adult Dave being driven off in a car, looking back at what he is leaving behind as he is being driven to his physical death. The finality of vigilante justice carries the same irrevocability as the crimes it condemns, the same compounding of human misery, the same emptiness of meaningless violence. In the end, vigilante justice simply perpetuates the violence it supposedly condemns in ceaseless cycles of sorrow. *Mystic River*, like *Unforgiven*, looks at the complexity of the human heart, asking for more just and more probing consideration of the heartaches and troubles in which we are enmeshed.

If vigilante justice is wrong, then what in fact takes its place? *Unforgiven* barely implies forgiveness as an alternative to violence; does *Mystic River* do any better? An interesting subplot within the film gives us a clue. It gives us a theme that will be picked up and developed further in *Million Dollar Baby*, and it has to do with an unexplained sin in the past of a main character. In *Mystic River* the character is Sean, the detective. Throughout the film we see him answering his phone, only to be greeted by silence. His estranged wife calls him but is unable to communicate with him. All we know is that a child has been born, but that Sean's wife left before the birth. Sean longs to be reunited with his wife and child, but he doesn't know how to break through her silence. Nor are we privileged with any knowledge of why she left. Was it his fault, her fault, their fault? "None of your business," says the film, which is only interested in letting us see resolution. It comes when Sean, sick at heart over the violence he observes in his job, feels his own inadequacy. He is a police detective, charged with preventing crime and solving crime. But the power of violence defies his own capacities to prevent or control it. And so when his wife calls once again, this time he confesses his inadequacy, names his own failure. And this time she responds. By film's end, she returns to him, and we see the three of them together at a parade—father, mother, child, reunited. Openness, honesty, and communication become all wrapped up as components in a forgiveness that offers a redemptive alternative to violence. And when we look back at the major plot of the film, we see how the inability to be open, to communicate, to acknowledge pain and inadequacy, has contributed to the movie's tragic ending. We begin to move beyond the simple assertion that violence is not the answer to violence. From *Unforgiven*, forgiveness; from *Mystic River*, forgiveness as involving honesty, openness, communication. These are the qualities we might weave into our positive constructions as we trace redemption in these two Eastwood films.

Sacrificial Love

The next two films, *Miillion Dollar Baby* and *Gran Turino* change course. Both still deal with the issue of violence, both struggle with ways to redress violence, but both take what might be called a Christian turn in their respective resolutions. We explore this turn, and query its role vis-à-vis *Unforgiven* and *Mystic River.* How do these later films challenge, supplement, or nuance the themes of violence and forgiveness in the two earlier films?

Whereas *Unforgiven* and *Mystic River* give us vigilante violence, *Million Dollar Baby* gives us controlled violence. Here our violent instincts are channeled into the sport of boxing. Our main characters are Frankie, Scrap, and Maggie. Frankie is the owner of a seen-better-days gym where he is also a trainer of boxers, and Scrap is his sidekick, and a fighter who trained with Frankie back in his younger days. Injuries Scrap sustained in his 109th and last fight cost him his sight in one eye. He now lives at the gym, and is Frankie's jack-of-all-trades. Our third main character is Maggie, a girl from Theodosia—a name that in Greek means "gift of God." Maggie comes from a so-called White-Trash family; she's made her way to Los Angeles because she's been a fighter from birth, and if Frankie will only train her, she knows she can be a champ. Boxing is a way for her to triumph over an otherwise deadbeat life.

Frankie finally agrees to train Maggie; and she does indeed go from win to win. During her fight for the title, however, just as she has turned back to her corner following a successful round, her opponent lashes out at her, knocking her flat. Maggie's neck hits the stool Frankie has just placed in her corner, and Maggie's spinal cord is snapped. This plucky fighter is now a quadriplegic with no possibility of recovery, able to move only her head. Following some months—and the amputation of a leg due to ulceration—she begs Frankie to take her off life support, and of course he refuses. She tries unsuccessfully to end her life by trying to bite off her tongue and so to choke on her blood, but her caregivers intervene. The film ends as Frankie comes to her at night, shuts off her life support, gives her a shot to quicken her death, and walks away.

What my brief summary of the film cannot convey is the depth of filial love that develops between Frankie and Maggie, and the depth of friendship love between Frankie and Scrap. In many respects, *Million Dollar Baby* is an unconventional love story. But there are two other aspects of the story that give it profound theological implications. Like Sean in Mystic River, who is estranged from his wife, Frankie is also a man who is unforgiven, alienated from his daughter Katie. As in *Mystic River*, so in *Million Dollar Baby* we do not know the reason for the alienation; we only see the results in Frankie's life. Early in the film we see Frankie at his nightly prayers: "Protect Katie," he asks, "and Annie too." Throughout the film he writes letters to his daughter; the letters are always returned unopened, with the cold "Return to Sender" stamped on the envelope. We do not know what lies behind this unresolved alienation. In the film *Unforgiven*, the refusal to forgive results in physical violence; in *Million Dollar Baby*, there is soul violence. The initiating sin is neither named nor explored; we only see a kind of resignation and continued pain as a result of the unresolved past. Nor do we know anything at all about Katie's life other than that her pain is such that she refuses all contact with her father. This film, like *Unforgiven*, does not tell us what forgiveness could be.

Another aspect that marks this film as a bit unique is its inclusion of the church. With a few notable exceptions, the majority of Hollywood films totally ignore the church. One would think that all life is totally secular, given the usual absence of religious symbols or communities in films. But in *Million Dollar Baby*, the church is almost a framing device. Early in the film, Frankie is coming out of church, arguing with the priest over the Trinity. For twenty-five years Frankie has been going daily to Mass, engaging the priest in endless theological questions, driving the priest up the wall. And the priest clearly knows his parishioner. "A man who comes to Mass every single day for twenty-five years is a man who needs forgiveness," he says. Near the end of the film, as Frankie agonizes over Maggie's request to stop her life support, we see him sitting in a pew, the priest beside him. He is asking the priest if he can accede to Maggie's request. No is the clear answer.

If you do this, the priest says, you will experience the worst soul loss possible. You will taste the despair of nothingness. But Frankie responds that he has been tasting such despair for the past twenty-five years.

The interesting parallel between our first two films and *Million Dollar Baby* is that in *Unforgiven* and *Mystic River*, killing is denounced as the way to resolve problems. In *Million Dollar Baby*, killing is an act of self-sacrificial love that resolves the problem. The first two films question death as the answer to violence, suggesting instead that forgiveness, openness, and honesty are involved in the answer to violence. But *Million Dollar Baby* and later *Gran Turino* complicate the answer. The denouement in this film poses a double death as resolution.

The priest has made it clear to Frankie, as he must given church doctrine, that to take Maggie's life will be a mortal sin that will plunge Frankie's soul into darkness. From this perspective, for Frankie to minister to Maggie's need will cost him a spiritual death—and he is a religious man. Even though the priest does not actually say that killing Maggie will result in eternal damnation, this is the cost so far as Frankie understands the situation. Maggie has made her needs clear. She has done in her life what she needed to do, achieving her goals in keeping with her wildest dreams. She experienced only rejection and greed from her mother and siblings, but through Frankie she has known a deep familial love; he is the father she lost as a child; she is the daughter he lost through alienation. Injured, Maggie is now an athlete who cannot move, whose limbs are being taken by gangrene. She has finished her life—and from her perspective, she has finished it triumphantly. She only needs cessation of these extraordinary measures that keep her alive against her will. To continue to survive is, to her, a living hell. She needs to die. And Frankie gives her the death she desires, even though he believes that by doing so, he will be plunged into eternal hell. He loves her more than his own soul.[1]

1. An interesting parallel exists in Shusako Endo's novel *Silence* (New York: Taplinger, 1980). A missionary priest in early seventeenth-century Japan must choose between apostasy and faithfulness to his vows. If he chooses apostasy

Frankie's relation to Maggie is paralleled by Scrap's relation to Danger, a young misfit of low intelligence who comes to the gym daily. Scrap watches over the boy, protecting him where he can, caring for him, letting him go when he must, welcoming him when he returns, almost like the father in Jesus's parable of the Prodigal Son. Scrap has a wisdom, patience, and love born from his own losses. Thus both Frankie and Scrap are seasoned through their own failures, affirming life in its ambiguity despite the losses, and finally identifying in love with those who suffer and struggle to be what they can be within the limitations of what they have been given. The love Frankie and Scrap offer to Maggie and Danger respectively is an empowering love that negotiates between control and protection, instruction and nurture. Each has survived anguish, dealing with it as challenge rather than defeat, and out of their own wounded survival, they give to others according to their need.

The theme of sacrificial love is repeated and expanded in the 2008 *Gran Torino.* Walt, played by Eastwood, is an angry man, still living the trauma of the Korean War. He is walled off from his neighbors by prejudice, from his priest by disdain, from his children by coldness. We first encounter Walt at his wife's funeral; we hear his insolent response to the priest, and listen with discomfort to his stream of stereotypical invectives against his new neighbors, a family of Hmong. The film entwines the stories of the teenaged children of the Hmong family with the story of Walt, inexorably leading to the film's denouement in the death of Walt for the sake of the Hmong teenagers.

An early incident has Walt saving the young Thao from the coercive efforts of a Hmong gang to join them. In the ensuing scuffle, the gang gets on Walt's lawn as well as Thao's. Walt appears

---

by stomping on the iconic face of Christ, the shogun will stop the physical torture he is executing on the priest's small flock, but the priest will be damned. If he refuses apostasy in order to save his own soul, his parishioners will die in agony. At the cost of his own soul, the priest stomps on Christ's image to save his flock—and so, paradoxically, even as he considers himself damned, he becomes most like the Christ who died that others might live.

with a shotgun and in Green Beret fashion gets them off his lawn. We practically hear the old Dirty Harry expression, "Make my day," as Walt challenges the young hoodlums to move out of his space. Walt has saved young Thao, at least temporarily, from his predatory cousin's gang.

The next rescue is of Sue, Thao's older sister. Walt has been downtown to get a haircut. Not so incidentally, the scene with the barber is set up to defuse Walt's abusive language: it turns out to be blue-collar code language for man-talk among friends. Stopping at an intersection, Walt sees the same gang molesting Sue. He drives up to the curb, threatens the gang with his tough talk, and has Sue get into the truck. Like Thao, she too is temporarily saved.

The Hmong family show their gratitude to a resistant Walt by bringing him food and flowers, which of course he rebuffs. Meanwhile, the gang has entangled Thao in their grip once again—this time away from Walt's support—and has told him he must steal Walt's prized car: an old, immaculately kept Gran Torino, as his initiation fee into the gang. Thao's options are to accommodate the gang or be continually beaten up. So Walt hears the noise in his garage at night, and stops the theft. The family says that Thao must make reparations by working for Walt for a week, a condition that Walt at first contemptuously refuses.

But later Walt sees an elderly woman across the street drop her groceries on the sidewalk as gang members pass by, laughing at her. Thao, who has also seen this, crosses the street, picks up the groceries, and helps the woman into the house. Walt's estimation of Thao goes up a notch, and he allows Thao to work for him. A bond begins to develop between the two of them. Walt teaches Thao workman types of things—including language—and gets the boy a job with a construction boss he knows. Through Sue and Thao, a mutual acceptance occurs between Walt and the Hmong family. But the gang will not let the family alone.

The critical scene occurs when Sue disappears. She has been kidnapped and brutally beaten and raped by the gang headed by her cousin. Walt is with the family when Sue, bruised and bloody, stone-faced and shocked, comes home. Because of Hmong customs, the Hmong family will not report the abduction and gang rape to the police. It seems there is no way to stop the gang's tormenting violence.

Meanwhile, Walt has learned that he has a fatal illness in his lungs. Knowing that he does not have many months left, he thinks about using his death as a probable resolution to the issue of how to stop the gang from viciously oppressing Thao and Sue. He knows that their whole future and perhaps even their very lives are endangered by the gang. But if the gang could be apprehended in a serious crime, with witnesses so that there would be nothing but prison ahead of them . . . and so Walt prepares himself for death. He buys a "burial" suit; he gets his hair cut; he does that which he has refused to do all these years: he goes to confession, confessing to the young priest who had officiated at his wife's funeral. And then he stands outside the home where the gang stays, and yells his challenge to them, vilifying them for raping and beating their own cousin. Neighbors come out and watch, witnesses to what will happen. The gang members have previously seen Walt with both a shotgun and a handgun. As they watch him, he asks if they have a light. "I do," he says, and reaches into his inside coat pocket. The gang members, of course, think he is going for a gun, and so they all immediately shoot at Walt, who is actually unarmed. As he dies, his arms outstretched, Walt's body falls to the ground and assumes the shape of a cross. The police have been called. They arrive and arrest the gang, whose members will now go to prison for murder. Walt has saved Thao and Sue.

But Thao, Sue, and even the priest have also saved Walt. We have seen Walt's dysfunctional relationship with his sons and their families, we have seen the walls he has built around himself. In his last confession to the priest, Walt confesses that he has not known how to be a good father to his sons, or how to deal with the violence forced upon him during his war years. Thao and Sue have broken through those walls with their persistent kindliness, and Thao actually teaches Walt fatherly skills in his own need for a father figure. The Hmong family has shown Walt how to be family, and incorporated him into their own. In this film, capped with an ultimate sacrificial love, each of the main characters participates in the salvation of the others, if we understand salvation to be forms of redemptive living. We each participate in one another's redemption.

The role of the priest in the film is instructive. He is present from the beginning, offering a gracious presence to Walt, which Walt ungraciously refuses. But the priest is not put off by Walt's rejection. The priest had made a promise to Walt's wife, he says, to lead Walt toward confession. Walt insults and denounces the priest, but the priest keeps coming after him. Given the explicitly religious nature of the film, the priest can be read as a metaphor for a God who persistently offers possibilities of grace, or paths of healing, even when the offers are persistently refused. The offers keep coming, always enabling the receiver to accept the offers, but always also accepting the receiver's decision. Rejection does not stop the continual offer of better possibilities for dealing with life's issues. In the film, Walt—redeemed through the love extended to him by his neighbors, a love that he learns to return—makes his peace with God through confession, and then performs his ultimate act of love in his self-sacrifice. The priest (like God?) is with him, all the way.

If we look at the trajectory Eastwood develops through these four films—*Unforgiven, Mystic River, Million Dollar Baby*, and *Gran Torino*—we see Eastwood first pinpointing the problem of our refusals to forgive one another, and the mayhem that follows such refusals. He suggests that forgiveness involves naming our own part in the problems we encounter to the ones we have harmed. The humility of such an attitude opens us to empathic identification with others—to love. Receiving and giving love to others, at whatever cost, creates a redemptive way of living that necessarily becomes communal in its nature. And the community is one of hospitality, giving and receiving care. This characterizes Frankie's relationship to Maggie, Scrap's relation to Danger, and finally Walt and the Hmong's family's relationship to each other. What *Gran Torino* adds is the mutuality involved in redemptive living. Participating in community is part of the redemptive process, insofar as we care for one another's well-being.

Looking back at *Mystic River* we can easily see how the lack of openness, communication, and care for the other's good contributes to the tragedy of Dave. Certainly this was so in the character of Dave's wife, but the same lack permeates the film, broken only by the subplot's resolution of Sean's marital problems. In *Unforgiven* we see such qualities in the friendship between Munny and Logan—but only there. It is lacking in all other relationships within the film. In a sense, both *Million Dollar Baby* and *Gran Torino* provide the communal dimensions lacking in the first two films. And yet it is these two films that utilize the violence of death, repudiated in the first two films, to resolve the issues.

In the first two films, death is punitive. The understanding of death as punitive echoes deeply in the Christian tradition. But in the second two films, there is nothing punitive in the two self-sacrifices that occur, despite the priest's caution to the central character in each later film. It leads a Christian theologian to ponder: have we unnecessarily attached punitive underpinnings to the cross, foolishly transferring human connotations of death as punishment to God? In the latter two films, death is given not to punish, but as the only way within the circumstances to offer release from suffering to the beloved. In both films, it is the ultimate expression of love. The challenge to a Christian theologian would be revisioning the meaning of Christ's death away from punishment and toward a deeper exploration of love in the midst of evil. The danger would be a valorization of death over life, whereas in both films death is for the sake of affirming life. This is so even in *Million Dollar Baby*, where allowing Maggie to finish her life at the same time affirms her choice and her stricken body's readiness for death. It's similar for Walt: his body has begun the process of dying. Walt chooses its time of death for the sake of the life which that manner of death can accomplish for those he loves. Self-sacrificial love is for the sake of life, not death.

Resolution

Given the dominant Christian motifs that emerge in these films, it seems natural that the final Eastwood film for our consideration is the 2010 *Hereafter.* The Christian tradition has always conjoined the notion of redemptive living in this life with a *more* that follows in a form of life beyond death.

Hereafter is more meditative and suggestive than Eastwood's other films, with the plot loosely woven around three different stories that predictably weave together in the final scenes. The focus is less on the three stories than on the intimations of life beyond death that each gives. One involves a French woman, a journalist on a Christmas vacation in Indonesia in 2004, where she is engulfed in the great tsunami that devastated so much of Southeast Asia at that time. Eastwood takes us into her trauma: the rushing waters, being swept up in the tidal flood, and the near-death experience as she momentarily experiences drowning. Suddenly the noise and turmoil of the tsunami recede, replaced with shadowy figures in a kind of dream world that inaugurates a different form of life following death. Then the film shifts again to the horror of the tsunami. Rescuers see her and pull her out of the waters, and resuscitation brings her back to life. Haunted by her near-death experience, she investigates accounts of similar experiences, and writes a book.

The second story involves a young American man who also died and was resuscitated, but the aftermath of his experience is that he is peculiarly sensitive to others in a psychic way. By touching another, he becomes aware of the other's grief and pain because of a loved one's death, and also of a communication coming from that loved one to the survivor. In every case, the communication is loving, deeply caring for those who still live. Other than this, the ongoing lives of those who have died are shrouded in mystery.

The third story involves a pair of young children in England who are identical twins, deeply connected to each other. One of the twins dies in a freak accident, and the other feels as if he has lost half of himself. He learns through the Internet about the psychic, and tries desperately to contact the psychic in order to hear from his dead twin brother.

Throughout the film, Eastwood suggests that the deep loves of this life persist beyond death. Just how this new form of love is developed, and what life beyond death is like, is left unstated. Eastwood gives first steps of life beyond death but leaves the further steps shadowy, intimated rather than explained. If *Hereafter* is looked at as part of the trajectory developed by the other four Eastwood films I have outlined, then the very tentativeness of *Hereafter* is part of its strength. There is more, Eastwood suggests, and that more involves love. Beyond that, we cannot and need not go. *Unforgiven* and *Mystic River* imply that redemptive ways of dealing with violence involve forgiveness; *Million Dollar Baby* and *Gran Torino* suggest that redemption involves sacrificial love, and *Hereafter* completes the notion by extending love into life beyond death.

Clint Eastwood, unlike five of the other directors considered in this study, has used scripts written by others, not by himself. (Ang Lee is the other exception.) Is Eastwood expressing his own vision as he works with each script, fashioning it into the presentation he has given us, replete with theological implications? Perhaps it is the case that Eastwood and his authors have simply absorbed the iconic values of Christianity into their thinking, projecting them unwittingly into a good story. We the viewers receive the stories, integrating them into our own stories, allowing them to enrich and question our stories in the ongoing adventures of our lives.

2

Woody Allen

Meaning, Morality, Mortality

Annie Hall (1977)
The Purple Rose of Cairo (1984)
Hannah and Her Sisters (1986)
Crimes and Misdemeanors (1989)
Matchpoint (2005)
You Will Meet a Tall Dark Stranger (2010)
Midnight in Paris (2011)

Woody Allen, an avowed agnostic, may seem an odd choice for a study of redemption in film. In many ways, however, Allen is one of the most theologically interesting filmmakers. While eschewing the notion of God, he nonetheless frequently refers to God as he explores the issues of meaning, morality, and mortality. Allen becomes a counterpart to Dostoevsky's famous dictum in *The Brothers Karamazov* that if there is no God, all things are permitted. If there is no ultimate moral structure to the universe, no final accounting for evil choices and deeds, is morality simply a social convention? A godless universe also holds implications for meaning. If there is no life beyond the one we are living, and death quickly blots out what little we have achieved, is meaning an illusion? Swallowed up in the immensity of endless times before and after our brief and insignificant flicker of life, our meanings are as ephemeral as ourselves. If God and some afterlife are essential to meaning and morality, then our mortality is a fearsome thing, an ultimate end with no ultimate God rescuing us from death. Woody Allen faces secularism in American culture with the stark consequences of the loss of God.

To trace Allen's trajectory in exploring these issues, I use seven films from the period 1977 through 2011, beginning with his iconic 1977 film, *Annie Hall.* This film and the 1984 *The Purple Rose of Cairo* show Allen wrestling with the problem of meaning. The next three films are *Hannah and Her Sisters* (1986), *Crimes and Misdemeanors* (1989), and *Matchpoint* (2005). Each of these films, with increasing intensity, deals with morality and mortality, with the issue of meaning never far behind. The hints toward possible resolutions in all five of these films are more fully developed in the final two films for our consideration, *You Will Meet a Tall Dark Stranger* (2010) and *Midnight in Paris* (2011).

Meaning

Annie Hall begins with Allen's character, Alvy Singer, talking directly to us, the audience, explaining the problems of relationship. We, the audience, are functioning in effect as therapist, the listener, the other who hears him into speech. We then move into episodes covering a year of Alvy's relationship with Annie, sometimes with flashbacks to Alvy's childhood. The episodes are not chronological, but they all drive toward attempts to understand life through relationship, specifically through a single relationship that holds the possibility of deepening one's personal meaning in an otherwise chaotic universe. Throughout the film, the viewer continues to function as listener, and the episodes recounted are the monologue that we hear.

Both Alvy and Annie move from vagueness to decision, but not in parallel lines. Alvy, having endured two clearly misfit marriages, is ambiguous and hesitant about committing himself yet a third time. He is a successful comedian and author. Older than Annie, he sees himself as shaping her, encouraging her, as a kind of Pygmalion who will bring her inchoate self into definition. But as Annie responds, instead of becoming the person Alvy envisions, she grows into a more self-assured woman of her own choosing. She changes from an insecure singer ignored by the diners in the club into a singer clearly in command of her audiences, attracting offers that will advance her career. In the penultimate scene, Alvy flies to hated Los Angeles to ask Annie to marry him. But Annie, having found her life, refuses. So Alvy returns to New York, writing his experience into his next play.

Throughout the film, endlessly telling one's story is a way to reshape the story, weaving it into a form of meaning that makes sense out of life. The meaning is less the result of the story told, and more the very process of telling, a process necessarily coterminous with life itself. In and through the telling, meaning is both created and experienced. Telling one's story is a kind of subtext to the actual living of life, infusing one's life with meaning and value. When Alvy fails to win Annie, his creative response is simply to turn that failure into a story: the play that he writes. Meaning, then, is not something that is set and given, not something come down from transcendent realms. Meaning is itself a variable creation emerging from the way one chooses to tell one's life. To make meaning out of one's life is endlessly to create it as story. The story is both wrested from and imposed upon chaos. It is as if there is a wild uncertainty about life, a randomness of one senseless thing after another, which would easily sweep us along, like a flash flood crescendoing down an arroyo. Turning the chaos into story is like finding a way to channel the wildness of the flood into an irrigation system. One's life is saved.

Story plays a similar role in *The Purple Rose of Cairo*, but in this film it is not the story one tells, but the story one is told—in this case, through film. The setting is the Depression of the 1930s, and Celia is a lonely young wife caught in a dreary marriage to an out-of-work bully. She compensates for his infidelities and abuses by losing herself in the movies that she constantly attends. We watch her sad face become transformed as she loses herself in the story the film is telling, until, after she has watched the same film day after day, one of the characters steps off the screen and approaches her. This is Tom Baxter, explorer and minor character in his film, evoked into life by Celia's devoted attention. In the midst of the audience's uproar over the untoward event, Tom Baxter whisks Celia out of the theater, and they go to a winterized amusement park where they can talk. Tom Baxter is an innocent, knowing only those things and qualities written into his character; Celia begins explaining the world to him. In one scene they enter a church; he admires its beauty.

"You do believe in God, don't you?" she asks.

Given his confusion, she begins to explain that God is the reason for everything. Tom, puzzled, listens, then has the "Aha!" moment: God is like the scriptwriters who put together the film! Celia counters that it's much bigger than that: God is the reason for everything; otherwise, life would be like a movie with no point and no happy ending. Illusion and reality, fantasy and hard knocks, are constantly competing in Allen's *The Purple Rose of Cairo*, and God is clearly placed in the land of illusion and fantasy. We are left with reality and hard knocks.

At story's end, Celia is disillusioned once again, back where she started. We see her return to the movie theater, sitting in utter dejection. On the screen Fred Astaire is singing about heaven (Allen's symbol of illusion) as he dances with Ginger Rogers. Slowly Celia lifts her downcast eyes to the screen, and we watch the gradual transformation of her face until once again she is rapt, transported through illusion to a place she can never attain, mediated not through telling her own life as story, but through identification with the stories of others.

If *Annie Hall* gives us the meanings that can be created in and through telling our stories, *The Purple Rose of Cairo* paints a tender but bleak picture where illusion is the only escape from a reality totally devoid of meaning. Rather than telling one's life as story, one forsakes one's own experience as much as possible in order to enter wholly into another's experience, another's story, which then functions as substitute for our own. In such a world, "life is like a movie with no point and no happy ending," and God is part of that world of illusion that keeps us from facing and dealing with life's problems.

In both *Annie Hall* and *Purple Rose of Cairo,* meaning is an elusive goal, and the role of story, one's own or another's, has a fragile place. In *Annie,* one's story must be heard if it is to ground one's meaning. There must be a therapist or an audience (or God?) through whom the story can be absorbed and bounced back; the film's ending has Alvy struggling to turn his failure into a play whose audience will redeem his failure. But in *Purple Rose,* the audience (in this case, Celia) is no answer; it simply compounds the problem. The audience, be it therapist or filmgoer, is an illusory ally. The therapist, the audience, or God only hears, never answers. There is no happy ending. We must wait for *You Will Meet a Tall Dark Stranger* for Allen's different take on the role of illusion in a godless universe.

Morality and Mortality

Our next three films explore morality in a world where the function of God is in the realm of illusion. We see the issue of God in a minor way in *Hannah and Her Sisters*; it becomes a major counterpoint to immorality in *Crimes and Misdemeanors*, and drops out entirely in *Matchpoint. Hannah* and *Crimes* use morality as major plot, and mortality as subplot. In *Matchpoint* the issue of mortality as well as the issue of God disappears, and the focus stays intensely on morality in a godless universe.

In *Hannah and Her Sisters*, Hannah is the successful figure, balancing an acting career, motherhood, and extended-family responsibilities in seemingly effortless competence. She is the wise sister, daughter, and wife: the one to whom others turn, and whom others resent and love simultaneously. The main plot revolves around the way Hannah's husband and sisters betray her.

The subplot directly deals with mortality and its implications for meaning. Mickey, a Chaplinesque character often appearing in Allen's films and usually played by Allen himself, is a neurotic hypochondriac. He is also a moderately successful TV producer, and the ex-husband of Hannah. His life is governed by his fear of death, a fear often driving him to doctors with minor complaints. When one such complaint leads to extensive hospital tests for a possible brain tumor, Mickey is plunged into despair, convinced that he is finally encountering his mortal illness. Following the tests, he is told there is nothing wrong with him. In a delirium of happy relief Mickey runs out of the hospital, leaping for joy—until he realizes that although he has come out all right this time, eventually death will be his fate. This plunges him into a morass of meaninglessness, and he turns to religious faith for a possible hope of surviving death. "If I can't believe in God," he says, "life is not worth living." Death blots out not only one's existence, but all possibility of any enduring meaning for the life one has lived.

We follow Mickey's comical turn first to Catholicism, then Hinduism. His misadventures in each case become the underlying subplot: how is one to find meaning, if death ends the entirety of one's life? Presumably only if one's life endures beyond death is life worth living. The issue is resolved later in the film. Mickey happens upon Hannah's sister, Holly; she tells him about a play she has written, and a romance begins. But by now Mickey has lost the frantic persona of his earlier hypochondriac scenes.

"What happened?" she asks, and he tells her that in the midst of suicidal despair, he began walking randomly through the city, ending up in a theater where an old Marx Brothers comedy was playing. In the course of the rauçous humor he gained insight into the precious quality simply of life itself. In the midst of trauma, there is comedy: existence is funny.[1] Laughing at the Marx Broth-

1. Allen is replicating a famous scene from a much earlier film, *Sullivan's Travels* (1941; written and directed by Preston Sturges). The Coen Brothers borrow from the same scene in *O Brother, Where Art Thou?*

ers film, he comes to the realization that the purpose of life is not some final meaning, but the sheer enjoyment of living itself. Perhaps there's more; perhaps there isn't. Essentially, it doesn't matter: life is worth living on its own terms. Just as the issue of illusion raised in *The Purple Rose of Cairo* will be revisited in *You Will Meet a Tall Dark Stranger*, so the entwined issue of mortality and meaning will be revisited and developed more fully in *Midnight in Paris*.

Meanwhile, in *Hannah and Her Sisters*, the subplot of Mickey's wrestling with life and meaning is woven back and forth with the intrigues of Hannah's husband and her sisters, Lee and Holly. Hannah's husband, Elliot, has begun an affair with Lee. Lee mirrors some of the same traits of Annie from Allen's *Annie Hall*. Like Annie, Lee is an insecure woman who has for the past few years been taken under the exploitive wing of an older man who will teach her all she should know and be, shaping her into his perfect counterpart. Tiring of this subservient role, Lee is easily seduced by Elliot. They begin an affair that is carefully kept from Hannah. Lies, evasions, and quick tempers now mark what had been Hannah's stable marriage.

If Lee deceives her sister Hannah, Holly exploits her sister's generosity. Holly, like Lee, is also insecure, but whereas Lee's insecurity drives her into the haven of a man's need for her, Holly's insecurity rests in her failed attempts to find a career. Hannah is her enabler, financing Holly's various efforts. In doing so, Hannah simply reinforces her own role as successful on both fronts: career and marriage. Measuring themselves against Hannah, Holly and Lee endlessly find themselves wanting. Resentment follows.

This is an Allen story where "all's well that ends well." After a year of deceit, Elliot and Lee end their affair, with Hannah suspicious but seemingly none the wiser. Lee, who has started looking to her own education, marries a fellow student, and Mickey and Holly (now a successful playwright) marry. But there is an uneasy morality, mirroring in its own less dramatic way the issues of mortality and meaning so dominant in the subplot about Mickey. This is a film where exploitation of others functions as norm: Lee's Pygmalionesque partner, Elliot and Lee's exploitation of Hannah's trust, Holly's financial exploitation of Hannah, and even hints of betrayals and exploitations in the lives of the women's parents. But there are no negative consequences for these exploitations and betrayals. Each is like a pebble thrown into a pond, causing rings but eventually reaching a terminus at pond's edge, with calm restored. Even so, *Hannah and Her Sisters* deals with the ripples of exploitation but resolves into equilibrium by film's end.

Crimes and Misdemeanors ups the ante, so to speak. If the moral issue is infidelity and exploitation in *Hannah*, the moral issue in *Crimes* is not only infidelity but murder. The protagonist in the film is Judah, a very successful ophthalmologist, and throughout the film "eyes" function as a metaphor: eyes as the windows of the soul, the eyes of God, the eyes of society in the way society "sees" life, the "eye" of the camera as it films life.

The film begins with Judah making a speech at the opening of a new hospital wing devoted to ophthalmology. He recalls the notion of the "eyes of God" filling him with awe as a child, and his subsequent fascination with eyes that led to his career choice. Now he is a scientist who has left behind the religious notions of his childhood.

We soon learn the moral dilemma in which Judah is caught: several years earlier he began a happenstance affair with Dolores, who turns out to be pathologically insecure. She demands that Judah leave his wife, which Judah under no circumstances will do. Dolores threatens him with her knowledge of financial improprieties he used while in control of funds for the new ophthalmology wing.

Judah confides in Ben, a friend, brother-in-law, and rabbi who is also a patient: Ben is going blind. Their two worldviews are clarified in the conversation. Ben, counseling Judah to confess to his wife, believes there is a fundamental moral structure to the universe, with real meaning and forgiveness and some kind of higher power. Judah, on the other hand, sees the universe as harsh, empty of value. In Ben's world, respect for one another, decency, forgiveness, and caring are in harmony with the universe; in Judah's world, these qualities are functional in facilitating communal life but have no higher value beyond this. Ben, who sees a world that God has suffused with value, is blind; Judah, with his more cynical view, has twenty-twenty vision.

As Dolores's demands to confront Judah's wife become more strident, Judah turns to his brother Jack for help. Jack, highly placed in the underworld, suggests murder. At first Judah resists, but in desperation he accedes. Jack arranges the murder, calling Judah to inform him when it is done. Judah goes to Delores's apartment, sees her on the floor with lifeless eyes open, soulless. Removing incriminating evidence of their relationship, he leaves.

Tormented with guilt, Judah visits his childhood home, and its present owner invites him in to look around, to revisit memories. In his imagination he sees a Seder meal in the dining room; an argument is in progress about whether or not there is a moral structure to the universe. Judah's aunt is belittling the notion of a moral universe and any notion that God punishes the wicked. Surely the fact of the Holocaust demands a different interpretation of the universe. Might makes right, and the winners write the histories. Judah's father counters that the wicked are indeed punished; God sees and judges all. When Judah's father is asked if he prefers God to truth, he responds that if necessary he will always choose God over truth, and in so choosing will have a better life than is possible for those who doubt.

Overwhelmed with guilt, Judah becomes moody, irritable, even tempted to confess his crime to the police. But after several months he awakes one morning: the sky is blue, the weather fine, he is surrounded by a loving family, he is esteemed in his profession and community. So he takes his family to Europe for a vacation, and the guilt is over: his successful life continues as before.

Once again, the Allen character's problems with meaning and death provide a counterpoint to the main plot. Clifford is the insecure character, this time a filmmaker working on a documentary about the inspiring life of an elderly philosopher, Professor Levy, who celebrates the meaning created in life through love. This seems to be a middle way between the indifferent universe of Judah and the God-infused universe of Ben. Professor Levy's view of God is anthropological; we humans create the concept of God, however clumsily. What endures are the values we create, which make life meaningful, primarily through loving relationships. But if this is a middle way in this film, the view is undercut by the end of the movie, as Clifford receives word that Professor Levy has committed suicide by jumping from a window ledge. His cogent arguments for life's meaning through love go out the window, along with the professor. We are left with Judah's universe, a pragmatic utilization of what means are available to create the lives we desire.

Matchpoint makes the point still more clearly. This film, made sixteen years after *Crimes and Misdemeanors*, drives the lesson home in the starkest terms possible. No longer do we have the counterpoint provided through Allen's usual character. We don't have a subplot at all. The film begins tellingly with a tennis ball teetering on the net, spinning; which way it will fall seems strictly a matter of chance. But for the players involved in the tennis match, the consequences of its actual fall can make the difference between winning and losing. Likewise, toward the end of the film a ring tossed toward the river falls short, and balances, spinning, on a railing. Which way it falls determines whether our protagonist gets away with murder. Chance and luck are driving forces in the game of life.

The tale is simple: the protagonist in this film is Chris Wilton, a tennis instructor of modest background who forms a friendship with Tom Hewett, a wealthy client. Through this friendship Chris associates himself with Tom's family, winning the affections of Tom's sister, Chloe. Unfortunately, Chris is compulsively attracted to Nola, Tom's sultry fiancee, who is also something of a social climber. Chris seduces Nola, and after his marriage to Chloe, begins a regular affair. As in *Crimes and Misdemeanors*, so in *Matchpoint* the mistress endangers the wealth and success that Chloe's father has secured for Chris in the business world, and so the mistress must go. And once again, this time in strange twists and turns, our hero defies fate and gets away with murder. In *Matchpoint* Allen gives us the stark consequences of a world in which chance and luck are the determining factors in a universe where morals are but matters of convention. Gone are the qualms of conscience plaguing Judah, gone as well are the philosophical musings on morality by Professor Levy. We are left with Ivan Karamazov's world, where without God, all things are possible.

Thus far, tracing the trajectory of evil and its resolution in the films of Woody Allen might seem to be a bleak process. But the very process of tracing a worldview to its ultimate consequences has great value. Allen takes us from the inept infidelities of *Hannah and Her Sisters*, through conscience as a battleground between moral and amoral views of the universe in *Crimes and Misdemeanors*, to the completely amoral world of *Matchpoint*. In the next two films, he backs away from an unmitigatedly coldhearted universe to one tempered with hope.

Resolution

You Will Meet a Tall Dark Stranger and *Midnight in Paris* pick up themes begun in the earlier films and flesh out what kind of a resolution is available in Allen's universe.

Allen explores the role of hope in *Tall Dark Stranger*, along with a form of religion that grounds that hope. He does so disarmingly by placing the source of hope not in a religious community but in a self-styled psychic, Crystal, who makes her living by spinning visions of a complex spiritual world. By building his story around a psychic, Allen can emphasize that the ground of hope does not lie in an objective reality that transcends the believer, but in the changes wrought within the believer through faith. Whether or not there are auras and past lives, as Crystal would have Helena believe, is beside the point. What matters is the change in Helena's expectations and attitude; these critical changes affect what she can experience. Helena's new expectation of a "tall dark stranger" gives her a quality of zest, curiosity, and hope as she meets new people, which of course enhances her attractiveness and invites attention. Expecting a new relationship, Helena is open to a new relationship. As this theme plays out in Allen's films, an idealistic, earnest character is like an island surrounded by a sea of hard-eyed realists. These realists see the world much like Elliot does in *Hannah*, as Judah does in *Crimes*, and as Chris does in *Matchpoint*. But in *Tall Dark Stranger* the realists lack the suave veneer of Elliot, Judah, and Chris.

The backstory to Helena's search for new life through the psychic is the destruction of her marriage to Alfie. Both are in their 60s; Alfie is in the grip of a late midlife crisis. He flees his marriage and its reminder of his own aging in the aging face of his wife, and he attempts to recapture his lost youth. All this lands him is marriage to a young prostitute who proceeds to empty his bank account and sabotage any of his ill-conceived hopes of being young again.

Meanwhile, Helena's and Alfie's daughter, Sally, is married to Roy, who struggles unsuccessfully to write his second novel. Roy in particular castigates Helena for her foolish faith in the psychic; she should be realistic and clear-sighted, like himself. But Roy ogles the lovely Dia, whose apartment window is just across from his; he romances her, divorces Sally, deceives Dia and her father with false information about himself and his prospects, and submits a stolen manuscript to his publisher as his own. Roy's end is shame and humiliation.

Sally, meanwhile, is also frustrated in all her hopes, whether for a career, for a family, for her marriage, or even for an affair with her boss. Sally too ends up frustrated and humiliated, and at her lowest point she castigates her mother for her foolish faith in the psychic. Thus as the film depicts Helena's move from despair to hope to fulfillment, it also chronicles the downward spiral of each of the characters espousing realism. They despise Helena's faith in the psychic even as they tumble relentlessly toward their own undoings. Allen's message seems to be that even though there is neither evidence for any moral structure to the universe, nor evidence of any sort of God beyond that existing within the imaginations of believers, still religious faith has a pragmatic function, no matter what form that faith may take. Faith itself may be a key to an optimistic approach to life that itself brings about optimal circumstances. Perhaps like a self-fulfilling prophecy, faith can create an attitude that brings about its own reward. Like Judah's father in *Crimes*, who prefers God to truth and considers himself blessed, Helena in *Stranger* opts for faith and winds up blessed.

In a sense, Helena's grasp on faith is reminiscent of Mickey from *Hannah and Her Sisters* as he flees to Catholicism and Hinduism. There the issue was mortality and the terror of nonbeing in death; Mickey frantically grasped at both forms of religion in an attempt to stave off the nihilism of death. Death pits the meaning of one's brief years of existence against an eternity of nonbeing; against these odds, our little lives are swallowed up, meaning and all, in an empty infinity. But against such an enormity, religion is powerless; Mickey rejects religion, and discovers instead the temporal joy of existence itself. Helena grasps at her own mode of religion, belief in the psychic's powers, not to stave off the meaninglessness of life in the face of death, but in order to find the courage to embrace life in spite of trauma. Whereas Mickey's use of religion yields failure, Helena's more modest use yields success. But in the final film for our consideration, *Midnight in Paris*, Allen revisits Mickey's experience once again in a strongly positive light. Mickey finally repudiated the search for life beyond death as an answer to meaninglessness. In *Midnight* this answer is reinforced.

Midnight in Paris begins with the camera moving from scene to scene within that wondrous city, almost like a travelogue. We move from one beautiful cityscape to another in sunlight, moonlight, and rain. This beginning to the film is a celebration of the city, of beauty, of existence. And then we are introduced to Gil, a character who, had the film been made much earlier in Allen's career, would have been played by Allen himself; but the character is here played superbly by Owen Wilson. Gil is in Paris with his fiancée, Inez, together with her wealthy parents. Gil is a successful scriptwriter who describes himself as a Hollywood hack; his deepest ambition is to write a novel, and he has indeed completed a draft. He loves Paris and dreams about what he considers its most vibrant era: the 1920s, when the city was a magnet for creative artists, especially from America. Gil nostalgically dreams of what it might have been like to live among them.

It is clear to the viewer that Gil's engagement to Inez is a mismatch, and indeed Gil's enchantment with Paris is countered by both Inez and her parents, who see the city as a postcard and a place where money might be made or spent. No magic exists in the city for them, and Gil leaves them as often as possible in order to explore the city on his own, always dreaming about the city as it must have been in the 1920s.

And then, with Gil sitting on the steps of a church as its clock strikes midnight, the magic begins. A 1920s-era cab appears; Gil is invited in and taken to a party by his newfound friends, who turn out to be Scott and Zelda Fitzgerald. He is, of course, transported to the 1920s, and his mind is fully boggled as he meets one idol after another.

Amid many twists and turns, Gil meets Adriana, who bemoans living in the boring 1920s; if only she'd lived at the turn of the century! A horse-drawn cab comes along, and Adriana and Gil go to Maxim's, and then to the Moulin Rouge. Together they meet artists such as Gauguin and Matisse. In the course of conversation, Gauguin decries his own time in history; the Renaissance, that was the period!

By this time it is quite clear that Allen is taking us back to *Hannah and Her Sisters* and to Mickey's revelatory experience that regardless of whether or not there is more to life beyond death, simply to exist at all, in whatever time, is fulfillment enough. What *Midnight* adds to this, lest we undervalue our own time, is that today's humdrum reality is tomorrow's nostalgia. The film becomes a celebration of life and a celebration of openness to all that life has to offer. To live at all is miracle enough, magical enough.

To trace a redemptive thread through these films of Woody Allen is to follow its unraveling in the messy challenges of life in a world without God. Is there meaning in such a universe, given the brevity of our lives? Does the overwhelming inevitability of the loss of ourselves and our meanings through death undermine the value of existence? Allen suggests that to succumb to despair is ridiculous, since despair blinds us to what is so abundantly given, the wonder of life itself.

What of morality? If there is no God, and there is no moral structure to the universe, is there any reason to be moral? Allen's stark drawing out of the consequences of an amoral life within an amoral world in *Matchpoint* is no endorsement of amorality as a way of life. In the earlier *Crimes and Misdemeanors,* Rabbi Ben and Professor Levy offer the alternative of living "as if" it were a moral universe in which our actions matter. However imperfectly this alternative is given, the lives of those who choose it are rich in honesty, in love, and in family relations. The elderly Professor Levy, despite his suicide, is given the final voice in *Crimes*: "We define ourselves by the choices we have made. Human happiness does not seem to have been included in the design of creation at all; it is only we, with our capacity to love, that give meaning to the indifferent universe."

And so mortality and morality cease to be issues. To embrace life in all its paradoxes and mysteries, and to dare to love, is enough. The alternative to despair is courage to appreciate one's time in all its fragile beauty, to be open to loving and being loved. Does this resolve the problem of evil? Is this redemption? Allen would no doubt eschew the term *redemption* because of its religious overtones. But if by redemption we mean a resolution of life's problems in ways that restore life's value, then Allen's working out of the issues is ultimately a redemptive answer. By no means does he stay with this answer: to the contrary, a subsequent film, *Blue Jasmine,* returns us to a world of neither meaning nor morality, to a world of only the emptiness of failure, as illusion crumbles beneath the weight of one's choices. It remains to be seen if Allen will return to the insights of these seven films. Whether he does or not, Allen's drive to question the issues of meaning, morality, and mortality in a godless universe is hard to surpass. His suggestive answers are pragmatic with regard to religion's possibly positive influence. Optimism and trust create conditions of thriving. And regardless of whether that optimistic approach to life is grounded in religion, such an approach becomes its own reward in providing zest and delight in the sheer joy of life itself. The issues of meaning, morality, and mortality cease to be problems. Instead, each issue serves as invitation to appreciate that one is, after all, alive to ask the questions.

3

Spike Lee

Doing the Right Thing

Do the Right Thing (1989)
Malcolm X (1992)
The 25th Hour (2002)
Red Hook Summer (2012)

TOWARD THE END OF Spike Lee's 1992 film, *Malcolm X*, Malcolm utters a line to a companion, almost as an aside. "Do the right thing," he says, and with this line Lee underscores the film's relation to his 1989 *Do the Right Thing*. Both deal with issues of racial violence; both probe ways of finding long-term resolutions amid short-term urgencies. Even though his 2002 *25th Hour* focuses on a White rather than on a Black community, in that film Lee continues to tackle the issue of racial prejudice and of striking out against those considered other. Ten years later, in *Red Hook Summer*, Lee once again includes the line "Do the right thing," this time in the context of the Black church. But that which is right is not always clearly discerned in the midst of human complexity.

Doing Right by the Neighborhood

Do the Right Thing takes us to a single summer day in Bedford-Stuyvesant during a heat wave: the temperature soars toward 100 degrees. The neighborhood radio DJ, who works behind first-floor windows that look out onto the street, opens the day and the film with his wake-up call and his music; indeed, the DJ functions throughout the film as a kind of unifying factor, calling the community to be community. The call letters of the DJ's radio station are L-O-V-E.

From there we are plunged into a day of increasing heat and increasing tension. Mookie, played by Lee, saunters down the street toward his job as pizza-delivery man.[1] The pizzeria is owned by Italian American Sal; he has been in the neighborhood for thirty years, watching kids grow up on his pizza. Sal's own sons, now young men, work the pizzeria with him. The older son is full of resentment and hatred toward the Black patrons of the store, while the younger son likes them, finding friendship with Mookie. Throughout the day during which it is set, the film both celebrates and critiques the community. We are introduced to three "cornermen" who spend their days by a brick wall painted bright red, alternately passing the time together in joshing conversation and in seething resentment and envy at the successful Korean-owned convenience store on the opposite corner. "They just got off the boat a year ago," the African American men complain, noting that nonetheless, here they are, succeeding in a business right in this neighborhood. In fact, other than the radio station employing the DJ we hear in the film, the only neighborhood businesses we see are run by folks who are not African Americans: the Korean American convenience store and the Italian American pizzeria.

Other characters include "the mayor," an older gentleman who favors Miller beer and who walks the streets of the neighborhood observing and commenting on the behavior of the young people. "Do the right thing," he advises Mookie on his way to the

1. In *Red Hook Summer*, made twenty years later, Lee as Mookie makes a cameo appearance, still delivering Sal's pizza.

pizzeria. The apparent wife of "the mayor" sits in a window all day, also observing the neighborhood, offering good advice to Mookie and others as they pass by. These two give the wisdom of the elders. We are also introduced to Radio Raheem, a young man thoroughly absorbed by rap music. "Fight the Power" blares from the boom box he carries. Smiley is a young man, probably with a mild form of cerebral palsy, who stutters and wanders up and down the street throughout the day trying to sell copies of the picture he carries. The women in the film, in addition to the woman watching from the window, are Tina, the Puerto Rican girlfriend of Mookie and mother of his son, and Jade, Mookie's sister.

An important character in the film is Buggin' Out (so named because of the thick glasses he wears). On this day when he goes into the pizzeria he becomes incensed that all the photos on Sal's "Wall of Fame" are Italian Americans. Where are the African Americans from sports, film, music, science, and politics? Why aren't they on the walls, since they represent the people of the neighborhood from whom Sal makes his living? Buggin' Out angrily asks the question (as he undoubtedly has before), and Sal runs him out of the place. Buggin' Out announces that he will incite a boycott of the pizzeria, but of course he cannot: the whole neighborhood frequents the pizzeria; it is part of their daily life.

The sultry heat and hot tensions of the day build until day's end. Sal is in the process of closing the pizzeria when a group of young folks ask to be let in for one more slice. He lets them in, and they are quickly followed by Radio Raheem and Buggin' Out. Both had been angered earlier in the day: Buggin' Out over the Wall of Fame and Radio Raheem because Sal had angrily insisted that the boom box be turned off if he wished to be served. Now the radio is blaring as Buggin' Out again loudly objects to the lack of African Americans on the Wall of Fame. Sal breaks the radio by repeatedly striking it with a baseball bat, and Raheem attacks him in retaliation. The fight moves outdoors; Raheem has Sal by the throat. As "the mayor" tries to pull him off we hear police sirens. A police officer pulls Raheem off Sal, as another handcuffs Buggin' Out. The officer has Raheem in a chokehold, pulling the nightstick ever tighter against his neck as another officer cries to him to let go, let go. But the officer keeps the hold; Raheem is strangled, falling dead in the street. The police drive off with Raheem and Buggin' Out in patrol cars. In the shocked silence that ensues, various people speak, and Sal says, "Ya gotta do what ya gotta do." Will the gathered crowd exercise its anger by attacking Sal? Mookie picks up a trash can and throws it through the pizzeria window. This galvanizes the crowd to vent its anger on the property rather than the proprietor; mayhem ensues as they all begin destroying everything in the shop. Smiley throws a lighted match, the shop begins to burn, all rush outside as the police and fire sirens wail. In the chaos, firemen turn the hoses on the crowd as well as the flames. By the end of the riot, with small flames still licking at the now burnt-out pizzeria, Smiley goes in and pins the picture he has been selling to the Wall of Fame. It is a photo of a smiling Martin Luther King Jr. and Malcolm X, shaking hands.

In the closing scenes, it is the next day. The radio DJ gives the wake-up call; Mookie is with Tina and his son in bed; he leaves while Tina is telling him to make something of himself. Mookie goes to the ruined pizzeria, where Sal sits heavily on the steps, and demands his pay for the previous week's work. Everything has changed, and nothing has changed. And we hear the radio DJ's voice commenting on the riot he had watched the night before from behind his radio window: we have to be community together, he says, or we won't be community at all; this is the LOVE station. And the scene fades as two quotations fill the now black screen. The first is from Martin Luther King Jr.: "Violence as a way of achieving racial justice is both impractical and immoral . . . impractical because it is a descending spiral of violence that ends in destruction for all . . . immoral because it seeks to humiliate the opponent rather than win his understanding . . . Violence is immoral because it thrives on hatred rather than love . . ." We are then given the second quote, from Malcolm X, who speaks about people being both good and bad, but the bad have the power to keep back things that people need. "Because of this, we have to preserve the right to do what is necessary to bring an end to that situation, and it doesn't mean that I advocate violence, but at the same time, I'm not against using violence in self-defense. I don't even call it violence when it's self-defense; I call it intelligence."

"Do the right thing." In Lee's film, the right thing is to stop the violence of racial hatred and injustice; the two quotes at the end of the film raise the all-important question of how this is to be accomplished. Indeed, at one point in the film Radio Raheem shows Mookie the brass knuckles he wears on the fingers of each hand: the fingers of one hand spell out *love*, and the fingers of the other hand spell out *hate*. As he folds his hand together, the two do not cancel each other out; rather, they are interwoven.

The violence in the film is a shared commodity. It is present in the seething racism of Sal's older son; it is also present in Sal, who has a love-hate relationship with his customers. It is present in the resentment built up in the community, whether passively in the cornermen's response to the Korean convenience store, or actively in Buggin' Out, Radio Raheem, and Mookie. But the violence so portrayed has a deeper and more invidious root in American society as a whole. For that, and to guide us in asking if transformation of violence is possible in the Bed-Stuys of our cities and towns, we need to look at our second Lee film, the 1992 *Malcolm X*.

Doing Right by the Nation

This 202-minute-long film proceeds in three parts: the first deals with Malcolm's family, beset and destroyed by the Ku Klux Klan and its brother organization in the north, the Black Legion. Malcolm's father has been murdered—beaten and tied to railroad tracks just before the train approaches; the insurance company calls it suicide, which of course means no payment. The children are taken away and put into various foster homes as the mother, unable to endure the pain, spends the rest of her life in an insane asylum. Young Malcolm is put "in his place" at school, despite his brightness. He drops out of school, becomes an addict and a petty criminal, and is sent to prison.

Part 2 gives us Malcolm's prison years and his conversion to Black Islam through the influential teachings of a fellow inmate and through a mystical experience during which he "sees" Elijah Mohammed, the leader in Black Islam. Malcolm forces himself to submission, Islam's key concept, and begins a life of intense discipline and study, even in the context of prison. He becomes Malcolm X, rejecting his earlier last name as a spurious inheritance from days of slavery, when slaves were stripped of African names and forced to receive the names of their masters.

The third section of the film takes us into Malcolm's life following release from prison. Elijah Mohammed, recognizing the strength and gifts of his young disciple, not only continues to teach him, but gives him the responsibility of establishing Islamic temples across the country. Under Malcolm X's fiery rhetoric, thousands of African Americans flock to Black Islam. Malcolm's message is separation from White America; he identifies the harshness and violence of racism with all Whites. Whether active or passive, a virulent racism underlies the entire structure of White persons and White society. Only by separating out from this evil can Black persons begin to identify their own strengths, become their own persons. If violence is necessary to fight the violence of racism, so be it.

But violence also emerges against Malcolm X within Black Islam. Malcolm X has continued his intensely disciplined life, renouncing all those things renounced by Islam. Almost to his despair, he realizes that Elijah Mohammed, his adored superior and father figure, has not embraced the same discipline he taught. His disillusionment, together with a murderous jealousy within the ranks of the ministerial circle of Elijah Mohammed, forces Malcolm to break away from the organization, and to start an Islamic society of his own.

He makes an all-important pilgrimage to Mecca, once again having a life-changing spiritual experience. This time he experiences the global reality of Islam, converts to Sunni Islam, and embraces the brotherhood of all races within Islam. When he returns to America, his message is tempered; he recognizes the alternative legitimacy of Martin Luther King Jr.'s nonviolent message, and modifies his previous separatist agenda. He endures increasing harassment from Elijah Mohammed's movement, and scarcely a year after his Mecca experience, he is brutally assassinated, presumably at instructions from Elijah Mohammed.

Malcolm X gives us the background to racism presupposed by *Do the Right Thing*. The overt violence conveyed through the scenes of first the Ku Klux Klan and then the Black Legion is supported by the pervasive cultural assumption of the inferiority of those whose forebears had been enslaved. Inferiority had become the justification for dehumanization, intensified by animalism that justified brutality against those whose humanity was not acknowledged. The spiral of slavery was the spiral of violence noted in the quote at the end of *Do the Right Thing* from Martin Luther King Jr.—a spiral creating "bitterness in the survivors, and brutality in the destroyers."

The racism spawned by slavery and then used to condone slavery corrupts the culture as a whole. To be born into a racist society is to imbibe its cruel values from infancy on, so that racism becomes the invidious norm of what is and is not acceptable. Such racism infects Blacks as well as Whites, inculcating assumptions of inferiority that hinder achievement. To transcend racism is at the same time to transcend violence, seeking transformation toward communities of well-being.

The films offer two resolutions. Malcolm X first espouses a complete separation from White society. But if racism is as invidious as suggested above, it has been internalized by its victims as well as by those born into privileged positions in a racist society. Racism corrupts the self-identity of its victims by breeding assumptions of inferiority within the self, undercutting the power of achievement or indeed, of even setting goals toward achievement. We see it epitomized in Mookie, who throughout *Do the Right Thing* is very invested in getting his pay—it is a recurring theme—but is not at all invested in responsibly carrying out the work that earns him his pay. His sister Jade, who holds a position selling watches in a department store, urges him to become "a man," which means to own his responsibilities. Her own success in holding a regular job, however, underscores the limits of achievement when one's intelligence is not valued enough to secure an education. She herself is kept to low-level achievements, denied the self-fulfilling work that an education might gain for her. All this underscores the problem: how does one separate from a racist society, when that very racism has permeated one's own sense of identity?

Malcolm X is a journey film, with that journey leading first to the destructive path of self-abhorrence, addiction, and crime; then toward self-respect and religious discipline through separatism. But the violence that ultimately kills Malcolm X depicts the insufficiency of separatism: the cruelty imbibed through racism erupts and kills; the separatists have not been able to separate from the killing power of racism within themselves. Racism hates the other, seeks dissolution of the other. And this is what murders Malcolm X through his Black brothers, even as it had murdered his father through the White racists.

Malcolm's journey, cut down by his assassination, moved beyond separatism as an answer. Through Sunni Islam he could break through his separatism by acknowledging White Muslims as his brothers and sisters. Upon his return home, he broke through his one-way approach by being able to find rapprochement with Martin Luther King Jr.'s nonviolent approach. And finally, he suggested an openness to working with Whites to overcome racism. Malcolm X had transcended the racism that had been inculcated within himself.

And what of violence? *Do the Right Thing* quotes Malcolm X's statement that violence in self-defense is intelligence. The biographical film includes Malcolm X's response to John F. Kennedy's assassination. Not only does Malcolm X condemn this act, but he also utters this "chickens-come-home-to-roost" statement quoted at the close of *Do the Right Thing*. That is, a violent society breeds more violence. His own assassination is grim confirmation of the insight.

If we turn to *Do the Right Thing*, violence yields destruction—the death of Radio Raheem, and the less horrible but still devastating loss of Sal's lifework. Sal can begin again; there is no new beginning for Raheem. And what of the community? The violence has offered a temporary release from the pressure of heat, tension, frustration, and envy, but violence has not brought about the good. No transforming value is accomplished. Nonetheless, Smiley puts the photo of Malcolm X and King on the destroyed Wall of Fame, and the DJ calls for a love that can transform a violent community into a community of mutual support, transcending the violence of racism within and racism without. The community, acting together, can become a means of transforming violence. Is this a sufficient answer?

Doing Right by Society

The film *25th Hour* probes the issue, now not within the context of the Black community, but within a mixed community in a New York neighborhood. The plot this time revolves around an Irish-American character, Monty, in the twenty-four hours before he must leave New York City to serve his seven-year prison sentence for drug trafficking.

The film opens with two pertinent scenes that reveal the ambiguity in Monty's character. Before the opening credits begin to roll, we are shown Monty and his cohort-in-crime driving, on their way to an important meeting. Suddenly, from the car in front of them, a dog is tossed from a window toward the pilings of the underpass. Monty immediately stops his car, against the protests of his buddy. The dog had been severely beaten as well as hurt from the fall, and at first Monty thinks he will shoot the dog, putting it out of its misery. But then, impressed by the spunkiness of the wounded animal, he decides to take the dog to a vet and to keep him. Next the opening credits roll, and the movie proper begins with Monty sitting despondently by the East River, the now healthy dog lying by his feet. A derelict druggie approaches Monty, begging him for a fix. But Monty angrily turns him away, telling him he's been "touched"—that is, caught, tried, and convicted. The wounded man parallels the wounded dog, but Monty is impervious to the man's plight. And in fact, as a drug dealer, he has contributed to his plight. So we begin with the two sides of Monty. Monty is compassionate and merciless both.

If we put this picture of Monty in dialogue with the statement by Malcolm X at the conclusion of *Do the Right Thing*, Lee confirms his assertion that we are not all bad, nor are we all good. Rather, human existence is a mixture of both, and the drama of human existence is the unfolding of these intertwined qualities. As we trace this unfolding in the story of Monty, the film next introduces us to the significant others in Monty's life: his two oldest friends, Frank and Jake; his live-in girlfriend, Naturelle; and his father, Brogan, a saloon keeper.

In each of these characters we see the same entwining of good and bad, albeit now within the thin borders of living within the law.

Frank is a Wall Street trader. His daily life veers between hope and despair as he plays the market in an intensely pressurized business. Jake, on the other hand, deals with different tensions, different hopes and despairs. He ploddingly teaches high school English to inner-city kids who show no real interest in the things Jake tries to teach. One lissome young thing, with a web tattooed around her belly button, offers him "favors" if he will change her grade—and Jake is both horrified and tempted. With regard to Naturelle, Monty's Puerto Rican girlfriend, we first see her in a flashback showing her teenage self on a swing in the park. In the flashback Monty stops to flirt with her; and now, in the present, we see her only as Monty's live-in girlfriend. We are told nothing of her life beyond this. Finally, we meet Monty's widowed father. Like Sal with his pizzeria in *Do the Right Thing*, this father has filled a wall of his saloon with famous faces. Only now the faces are those of firefighters lost in the 9/11 disaster.

The action of the film takes place on the evening before Monty goes to prison. Frank, Jake, and Naturelle accompany Monty to a party on his last night of freedom. A tension developing through the film is Monty's suspicion that Naturelle turned him in, but rather than confront her with his suspicion, he allows the distrust to erode their relationship. During the night, Monty learns that it was his drug cohort rather than Naturelle who fingered him. Frank, in a tense discussion with Naturelle, points out that each of them has benefited in one way or another from Monty's illegal activities. Her expensive clothes and jewelry, the fine apartment she shares with Monty—all have been purchased through drug money; all have been purchased through the misery of others. And neither Naturelle nor Frank nor Jake ever seriously attempted to turn Monty away from his lucrative involvement in drug trafficking. Each of them is complicit in the misery symbolized by the broken drug addict seen at the beginning of the film.

This theme continues to play out in a scene between Monty and his father, Brogan. Prior to attending the party, Monty visits his father in the saloon. They sit together in a booth, and Brogan apologizes for the neglect Monty experienced as a child, not only through the death of his mother, but also through the effective loss of his father, who turned to alcohol and work to cope with his grief, neglecting the child Monty. Brogan suggests that this neglect led to Monty's choosing the quick money, of involvement in the drug trade. Brogan acknowledges that he knew that money Monty had given him to meet his debts was drug money. Brogan also owns that in accepting the money, he has been complicit in its gain.

In this film wrongdoing is individual and corporate at the same time; its effects are weblike, spreading well beyond the point of impact. In this web, guilt is less an either/or option of guilt or innocence and more a matter of degree. To participate in the system of ill-being is to share the guilt of that system, whether or not one is legally indictable. The Christian parallel is the ancient but long dysfunctional doctrine of original sin. Like this film, this doctrine suggests that sin is social as well as individual, and that insofar as we are born into systems that perpetuate ill-being, and do little or nothing to challenge or change such systems, then we participate to some degree in the guilt entailed by those systems.

A scene immediately following Monty's conversation in the saloon with his father echoes the earlier two Lee films. Monty excuses himself, and goes to the men's room. As he stares at his face in the mirror, he begins to curse the luck that has brought him to his sorry state. In the process, he bitterly names all the separate groups in multiracial New York, cursing the African Americans, the Korean Americans, the Chinese Americans, the Arab Americans, the everyone Americans who comprise New York City, cursing all of them, rich and poor and native-born and immigrant, for his downfall. Finally Monty, exhausted by his tirade, stops speaking. He continues to stare at himself in the mirror, and then confesses that his troubles are not the fault of these others, but are his own fault. He is the one who made the decisions that took him to this point in his life. And he goes back to his father and then to the farewell party.

The film's major challenge lies primarily in its ultimate climax and resolution. Spike Lee gives an artistic nod to *The Last Temptation of Christ* in the closing scene.[2] In that film, Christ is tempted off the cross by a devil disguised as an angel, who tells him his very acceptance of the cross is all God requires; now he may come down, marry, and live a normal life. Many years later, Christ is visited again by the angel and learns to his horror that it is the devil. Suddenly we are shown Christ again on the cross, living toward his death. He will not come down. And so Monty's father drives him in the twenty-fifth hour to prison. As they drive, his father suggests an alternative: instead of driving to prison, they will drive across the George Washington Bridge and head west.

His narrative of what can happen is illustrated on the screen. We drive across the bridge, across New Jersey and Pennsylvania, passing a broken-down bus by the side of the road, which reads, "Christ Is the Answer." As we drive through middle America into the west, crosses appear here and there in the passing scenery. The final destination is a town in a faraway western desert state. There Monty says goodbye to his father and begins a new life. Eventually

2. *The Last Temptation of Christ* (1988), directed by Martin Scorsese.

Naturelle comes to join him; they marry, have a family, and then we see Monty gathering his children and grandchildren around him, revealing to them his secret past. But they are together and exist as family precisely because Monty took that alternative, rejecting prison, beginning a new life in the west. At that point we are abruptly returned to the car still on this side of the George Washington Bridge, just as in *Last Temptation* we are returned once again to the cross. Monty chooses to pass the bridge: he chooses prison. And the film ends.

The film insists that the way of redemption does not entail ducking the consequences of our crime but dealing with those consequences. Frank, Jake, and Naturelle must face their own complicity in Monty's guilt, and Monty himself must accept responsibility and its consequences. What is gained? Monty gains a continuity with his past that would be denied him were he to give in to the temptation to begin life anew. Monty is a New Yorker in his bones; he belongs to and with the people of that city, and by accepting prison, he accepts the right to return to his city after serving his sentence. Salvation lies not in escaping the consequences of one's wrongdoing, but in accepting responsibility and looking for creative ways to deal with those consequences that still might contribute to the common good.

The broken-down bus in the escape fantasy suggests that vicarious punishment as an answer to our ill-doing no longer gets us anywhere. Whereas Clint Eastwood in *Gran Turino* illustrates vicarious atonement, Spike Lee in *25th Hour* calls vicarious atonement into question. Lee's film suggests that beginning anew does not happen through a radical break with our past, but through dealing constructively with that past, even when its consequences entail severe punishment. In a sense, the only new beginning that counts for Monty is being able to return to his people. This is evident through several riveting scenes in the film. The first such scene takes place in that restroom in his father's bar, where Monty rails against all the people of New York for his plight, finally admitting that he, and not those others, is responsible for the choices he has made along the way. The second is the scene showing Monty and his father as they begin their drive to prison. During the drive, suddenly the sidewalks are lined with all those against whom Monty had railed in the saloon, but now they appear as his smiling friends, bidding him affectionate goodbyes and waiting his return. These are his people, Monty's people; he belongs to them and they belong to him. A bus comes by, and a Black child smiles at him from the window, writing his name, "Tom," on the misty bus window. Monty in return writes his name, "Monty," on the mist of his car window, and they grin at one another. Beginning anew cannot be leaving these people, this past. To be meaningful, any new beginning must entail embracing these people in new, more responsible ways.

Doing Right by the Victim

Red Hook Summer takes us back to the Black neighborhood in Brooklyn encountered in *Do the Right Thing.* A middle-class African American woman is bringing her twelve-year-old son to spend the summer with his grandfather, Enoch. It's not clear whether young Silas, who calls himself Flik, has ever met his grandfather before; relations between Enoch and his daughter are strained at best. She barely speaks to her father before leaving her son at his doorstep.

Enoch is pastor of Lil' Peace of Heaven Baptist Church, and the first two-thirds of the film center on the double role the church plays in the community. On the one hand, it is a place of emotional safety, but on the other, it offers more than it can provide for young people in search of meaningful lives. Opportunities for education and work seem to be no more available for the African American community in Red Hook than they were in *Do the Right Thing* twenty years earlier. The current community still suffers from losses incurred during the AIDS epidemic; older teens still make their way by dealing in drugs, poverty still plagues the community. We watch young Flik, straight from an affluent middle-class neighborhood in Atlanta, negatively value what he sees in his grandfather's city, including his grandfather's church. He is embarrassed by his grandfather's attempts to draw him into the religious life of the community.

Just as we assume that the film will take us through the summer by focusing on the friendship between Flik and Chazz, his newfound friend from his grandfather's church, Lee astonishingly changes the agenda. The film is far more than a story of the tender innocence of early sexual awareness, and more than a story resolving family problems. Instead, we are plunged into the effects of child rape by clergy. The scene is a church service. Enoch is passionately preaching. "Put down that reefer, put down that bottle," he says. "God is on his throne watching, making sure you do the right thing." A stranger named Blessing has come into the church, and has taken a seat in the last row. When Enoch gives the altar call, Blessing comes forward, his face twisted with emotion. Enoch approaches him, arms out in welcome, when the stranger spits out his accusation. Two decades earlier, when Blessing was a twelve-year-old boy, his pastor, Enoch, had molested him. Enoch fled Georgia in disgrace, eventually finding solace as pastor in Red Hook, where no one knew his history. The molested child, grown and bitter, spent fifteen years tracking down Enoch, and now he will have his revenge. The congregation erupts in pandemonium; the ushers try to remove Blessing from the church, but Blessing escapes their grasp, leaps over the pews to Enoch, and beats on him. Nine-one-one is called, and the scene shifts. Enoch is stumbling home, Flik beside him.

We are back in Enoch's apartment, Enoch sitting beside Flik.

"Is it true?" asks Flik. "Is it true what that man said?"

Enoch responds, "I got something I want to tell you. They built this place in 1938 for the dock workers, seven thousand of them, and then they stuffed the poor here: the Irish first, the Italians, the Blacks, and the Puerto Ricans. Folks was supposed to use this place as a stepping-stone, and there was no place to step to because they gave it all away. So now you are part of the problem; you're poor, and you're a drag on the very society you helped build up. You hide inside your problems for years, forever. I came here to hide. But there was so much beauty, it didn't seem like a punishment. God knows your deepest, darkest secrets, God turns his light on you."

Enoch continues by confirming Blessing's accusations, and telling Flik "I was a sick man, but God cured me, and what he didn't do I did with a doctor's help. After fifteen years I'm fixed . . . I got nothing to hide no more."

Enoch returns to the church to clean up the mess; while there, he kneels on the mourner's bench before the altar. The older teens we met earlier in the film enter the church and bitterly accuse Enoch, not only of his crime, but of harsh disillusionment. All around them, the leader says, they see ruined lives and no prospects for change, but at least in the church there were two models of goodness: Deacon Zee and Pastor Enoch. Deacon Zee was a drunk, and now Pastor Enoch is a child rapist. And the young man speaking for the group savagely beats up Enoch.

The last scene in the film shows Enoch taking Flik in a taxi for his return to Atlanta. Chazz shows up just before they leave, giving Flik the cross she has always worn around her neck. And Flik gives her his cherished iPad2. Signs of hope, of "life goes on"?

What are we to make of evil and redemption in this film, and how does it relate to Lee's earlier work? The evil is both social and personal. Just as it is in the other three films, evil in *Red Hook Summer* is enmeshed in "socially acceptable" poverty, in lack of opportunity, and in discrimination. The films *25th Hour* and *Red Hook Summer* add the dimension of personal guilt to the social dimension of guilt. Both personal and social guilt require personal acknowledgement of guilt. Beyond this, *Red Hook Summer* explores the tragedy for the perpetrator as well as the victim of child molestation. How do we "do the right thing" against powerful inner urges that go so contrary to the right thing? Is confession sufficient? The answer is clearly no. Confession does not undo the harm done; it does not bring back innocence to the molested child. Blessing cannot recover the inviolate state seen in Flik and Chazz as they sense the overtones inherent in their friendship. Enoch contextualizes his situation with the monologue about the social history of the projects, but the contextualization does nothing to explain away his crime. Neither do the successive beatings he receives in any way atone for his actions. Confession is not sufficient.

All that Lee finally gives in resolution is the community itself. The community also knows disillusionment. Reference is made in the film to the fact that we now have a Black president in the United States, but nothing changes in the lives of those in Red Hook, except the negative fact that now the residents are being crowded out of their own homes by the creeping gentrification of Whites returning to the city. Lee indicates this through a repeated scene of Chazz and Flik writing their names in the new cement of a sidewalk in front of a gentrified home—once a home for poor Blacks, but no more. A White woman dashes out the door, screaming at the children, chasing them away. Change is not for the better. But even in disillusionment and hopelessness, there is understanding and care for one another. Enoch will not be chased from Lil' Peace of Heaven, even though the mystery that the parishioners had sensed is now uncovered.

All four of Lee's films discussed here point to the importance of community if we are to transcend violence, transforming it to something better. *Do the Right Thing* pointed toward bonding together in the community of one's own kind; *Malcolm X* journeys beyond this in Malcolm's embrace of Martin Luther King Jr. and his new openness to working across racial differences. Lee's *25th Hour* spans those distances: it takes the viewpoint of a White Irish American enmeshed in the violence of drugs in order to speak of his transformation, not only through his owning his responsibility, but also owning his participation in the wider community. Whereas the earlier two films in their grim depiction of racist society show how we all imbibe racism to our ill, *25th Hour* begins to show a wider participation in community. We are each responsible for contributing to communal well-being. *Red Hook Summer*, returning to Black experience in Bedford-Stuyvesant, builds on the communal emphasis: together we can transcend the violence that so deeply entwines its coils within—but only together. Together we gain the strength to acknowledge our participation in guilt; together we gain the strength to accept what consequences we must; together—across all boundaries—we gain the power of community. By transforming the stuff of violence in the creation of community, we might finally be able to do the right thing.

4

Joel and Ethan Coen

Implacable Evil and Absurdity

Fargo (1996)
O Brother, Where Art Thou? (2000)
No Country for Old Men (2007)
A Serious Man (2009)
True Grit (2010)

WHETHER THROUGH COMEDY OR tragedy, lighthearted forays or desperate dramas, the Coen brothers probe various responses to human dilemmas. We explore five of their films: *Fargo* (1995), *O Brother, Where Art Thou?* (2001), *No Country for Old Men* (2007), *A Serious Man* (2009), and *True Grit* (2010). These films explore existence variously as absurd, rational, or simply ambiguous, and each film contrasts a sort of fundamental human decency with what also seems to be a fundamental human bent to destroy the good. Destruction can be callous, unwitting, or cleverly contrived to subvert others, presumably for one's own gain. By taking these five films together we follow the questions suggested by the Coen brothers: What are the basic human dilemmas? What, if any, are the ways of resolving these dilemmas? What is their theological import?

Decency

In *Fargo*, we are given a graphic account of violence. Jerry, a weak man bullied by his wealthy father-in-law and desperate for money, devises a scheme in which he will hire two ne'er-do-wells to fake a kidnapping of his wife, Jean, asking her father for an eighty-thousand-dollar ransom. Since the ransom request is mediated through Jerry, in reality he sets the ransom price at one hundred thousand dollars, thinking he will keep twenty thousand for himself prior to dividing the rest of the money with the kidnappers, at which time Jean will be safely returned. So goes the setup of this tense drama, where bad becomes steadily worse. Carl and Gaear, the kidnappers, manage to kill a state trooper as they are driving off with Jean in the snowy night, and so we have one death. A car passes on the lonely road as Carl is lifting the dead trooper, so he drops the trooper, leaps back into the car, and Carl and Gaear speed after the other car, which skids and crashes. They kill the boy driver and his girlfriend: now there are three deaths. Eventually Wade, Jerry's father-in-law, brings a briefcase with the ransom to a rooftop parking lot where Carl is waiting. Carl shoots Wade, who also shoots Carl, grazing his jaw with a bullet. The enraged Carl fires several more bullets into Wade's head, and also kills the parking attendant on his way out: that makes five deaths. When Carl stops to count the money, he discovers the extra twenty thousand dollars and hides it under the snow for himself, bringing the $80,000 to the cabin where Gaear is holding Jean. But Gaear has killed Jean, the sixth death. In an ensuing argument over money, Gaear kills Carl, and proceeds to stuff his body into a woodchipper—the seventh death.

The counterpoint to all this mayhem is the simple goodness of small-town people, most notably Marge, the seven-month-pregnant police chief who investigates the situation. The camera takes us back and forth between the carnage being dealt by the villains, and the townspeople's laconic speeches. Eventually a lead directs Marge to the lake cabin where Jean has been held and murdered; Marge arrives as Gaear is pushing Carl's leg into the woodchipper. The heavily pregnant Marge lumbers down the hillside to shouting distance, draws her gun, and arrests Gaear. As she is driving him handcuffed to jail, she incredulously recites the mayhem that has occurred, "and for what?" she asks, "A little bit of money . . . and here you are, and it's a beautiful day . . . I just don't understand it."

This last reference to the day sparkling white with the beauty of fresh snow, aptly bespeaks the metaphorical use of the landscape throughout the film. Like a snowball, violence simply grows, with one evil leading to and being surpassed by the next. Jerry's fearfulness and fretfulness drive his need to appear successful to his father-in-law; he has covered his failures in managing his father-in-law's car sales lot for as long as possible, and now money is due. So he dreams up his scheme, thinking it will get him money without his having to crawl for it. But the violence of what he considers a sham kidnapping quickly escalates through random chance and quick tempers to one murder after another. Like a light snowfall turned into a blizzard, the increasing violence goes beyond his control. Attempting to escape the fury of its storm, he flees town, but he too is captured by the police. Violence by its very nature bursts its boundaries, engendering more violence.

Fargo focuses single-mindedly on the connection between violence and greed. In this film, greed is variously a rapaciousness born of weakness; a need to control; and plain, old-fashioned lust. Jerry's need for money is to cover his ineffectualness, to deflect his father-in-law's scorn. He exercises greed through duplicity, whether in his regular business dealings, the ill-fated kidnapping plot, or his plan to deceive the kidnappers by keeping the extra twenty thousand dollars for himself. His father-in-law also manifests greed—by flaunting his power through wealth, by controlling others through giving or withholding money, by refusing to allow Jerry a share of the profits from his car dealership. And, of course, the kidnappers live through greed, whether for basic sexual satisfaction or for someone else's money, regardless of whether that someone else is the targeted victim or another of the kidnappers. Greed underlies the violence, and is in fact the root of violence. Greed gorges itself, obliterating the good of others in a focus on its own endless desires. And while the kidnappers are the focal point for the violence of murder, Jerry and Wade just as surely exercise their own forms of violence—Jerry in his total lack of concern for his wife's suffering, Wade in his cruelty to Jerry, and in the seeming grim pleasure he takes in the mental suffering he causes Jerry. The film is a study in violence driven by greed.

And does *Fargo* give us a resolution to violence? In a sense, the resolution is in the counterpoint of simplicity, honesty, and acceptance of one another. Close to the final scene, Marge and her husband, Norm, are in bed for the night. Norm tells Marge that his submission of a drawing in a postage-stamp competition has won acceptance for the three-cent stamp. Marge, who has just apprehended a murderer at some risk to her life and therefore to the life of the child within her, glows with pleasure at Norm's accomplishment. She tells him that three-cent stamps are important: people always need them when the postal rates go up. Norm grins sheepishly, pats her stomach, and says "two more months!" and they hold hands. It is as if the simple goodness and faithfulness of their relationship has kept the evil outside them, covered by the infinite snow, just like the buried money. The snow that was a furious blizzard for the perpetrators is instead a glorious sun-sparkled winter landscape for Marge.

Comedy

O Brother, Where Art Thou? counters the deadly seriousness of *Fargo* with lightness and humor. The Coen brothers ostensibly modeled their movie on Homer's *Odyssey*, and indeed, there are easy parallels to the Lotus eaters, the Cyclops, the Sirens, and other memorable moments in Ulysses's travels. But *O Brother* is also modeled on a classic film directed by Preston Sturges, in

1941, *Sullivan's Travels*. This film concerns a wealthy director, Sullivan, who decides to produce a tragedy called *O Brother, Where Art Thou?* reflecting the troubles of the depression years. Sullivan's colleagues deride and challenge him. What does he know of trouble, living in wealth as he does? And so in order to understand trouble, Sullivan pretends to be a hobo, but he is followed by a luxury trailer ready to meet his every need. Through a good deed gone wrong, however, he becomes the thing he pretends to be. He experiences injustice, torture, and imprisonment on a chain gang. The gang is taken to a picture show featuring cartoons. Sullivan finds himself joining his fellow sufferers in uproarious laughter at the cartoon antics. And he realizes that comedy, not tragedy, is the way to address life's ills. This film becomes a prologue to the work of the Coen brothers in 2001 as they proceed to make the very film that the fictional Sullivan considered and then abandoned, signaling this dependence by the title: *O Brother, Where Art Thou?* The reference is then immediately followed by the reference to Homer, as the key passage is flashed starkly on the screen. And then the Coen brothers proceed to weave both predecessors into their own telling of a tale.

Our hero in *O Brother* is Ulysses Everett McGill. He and two cohorts break loose from a chain gang and begin their adventures as Everett travels back to Ithaca, Mississippi, in order to prevent his wife Penny from marrying one of her suitors. Their encounters along the way include Homer's Teresias in the form of an old, blind man who tells them their future; an upstart boy straight from *Sullivan's Travels*, who rescues them from a flaming barn; the lotus-eaters portrayed as a Baptist choir going down to the river for baptism; a young Black man, Tommy, who plays a mean fiddle (in exchange for his soul, he says); three sirens who turn one of the men in for bounty; a Cyclops Bible salesman; the bank robber Baby Face Nelson; a Ku Klux Klan meeting with a *Wizard of Oz*–style rescue of Tommy; and a Javert-like marshal determined to string the guys up. Throughout, the film is accompanied by winsome mountain music.

As a fulfillment of *Sullivan's Travels*, *O Brother* contrasts good and evil in comic rather than tragic mode. There is real evil: manipulation of relationships for financial gain, the relentlessly pursuing marshal, the horror of the Ku Klux Klan readying itself for a ritual killing, and the self-aggrandizing politicians. There are also the haunting themes of the human spirit in songs such as "Hard Time Killing Floor Blues," "O Death," and "Lonesome Valley." But goodness predominates: in the growth of genuine affection for one another within our trio; in kindness from strangers; and in a society where, for the most part, people pull together. Overall the theme is one of hope on the journey home, of finding a way out of no way, of finding treasure in unexpected places. Evil is recognized. It simply is denied the last word. "I am a Man of Constant Sorrow" may be true of the human condition, but it is also the song that wins the day for Ulysses Everett McGill and his cronies. Evil and hard times are recognized but denied their finality in comedy.

O Brother communicates not simply through the story line, even with its rich allusions to classical and Depression-era mythologies, but also through music and mood. In a nighttime scene the three cronies plus Tommy the fiddler are sitting around a campfire as Tommy sings and plucks "Hard Time Killing Floor Blues." The camera studies the faces as Tommy sings his lonesome song, and the faces of the characters are studies in hard times and hope. Wistfulness, loss, possibilities: there are no words, just the song and the faces in the flickering firelight. There is transformation and redemption as our heroes constantly escape certain death in each of their escapades, and finally achieve an official pardon from the governor. Ulysses Everett (maybe) wins back Penny and his daughters. But of course the real transformation in the film concerns the exchange of the constricting bonds of prison to the freeing bonds of friendship and the ability to look hard times in the face and find something funny anyhow. With regard to the first theme, as Everett explains it, the only reason he concocted a story that would bring Delmar and Pete along with him on his escape was the fact that the three of them were chained together. Everett could only leave if they all left. And, indeed, in the first half of the film mistrust and suspicion mark the relationship. But trust, affection, and loyalty emerge. Delmar is desolate over the loss of Pete, cherishing the horned toad he thinks was once his friend. Pete agonizes over the fact that he saved himself from a hanging death only by revealing the destination of his friends. Everett risks recapture by leading the bold rescue of Pete. And the three of them risk their lives to save Tommy from the Klan's lynching gallows. Chains of iron hold them together in bitterness and mistrust at the beginning of the film, and the journey toward the treasure is the forging of softer bonds, uniting bonds, the paradoxically freeing bonds of friendship.

The major thesis of *O Brother, Where Art Thou?* seems to be that the response to the tragedies of life need not be bitterness, need not be revenge, need not be despair, need not be cynicism. Rather, there is a kind of transcendence of tragedy offered through humor and through music. With regard to humor, this is not a matter of cracking some shallow joke to break the tension; it is not a denial of tragedy through a forced cheerfulness. Rather, it is as if there is a joy deeper than all our tragedies down in the depths of things, something bespeaking a deeper truth than our distortions of one another's well-being; something in the way of things that laughs and invites a joining laughter. There is a kind of attunement to these depths that brings about a crack in the brittle crust of evil, creating a sort of fissure in the tragedy where deep and joyous laughter can bubble up. The laughter doesn't make the tragedy go away—some tragedies are simply with us. But the laughter gives a transformation in the midst of tragedy, and this in turn gives endurance that itself can take us yet further into the journey of human caring and richness of spirit.

Music parallels this gift of humor, creating the same effect in its own way. Tragedy clings to the limp, thin skirts of poverty, whining for consuming attention, whispering of debilitation, despair. But music sings the tragedy, lifting it and transforming it into the beauty of song. From the song "I Am Weary, Let Me Rest," the call to "kiss me, Mother; kiss your daughter" refuses the dreary death through poverty, insisting upon the richness of the connecting kiss, the persistence of love, the triumph of thick hope. At every turn in the story, music offers the counterpoint to humor, echoing laughter with warm beauty. It is no accident, of course, that "I Am a Man of Constant Sorrow" is the song that resolves our three heroes' fortunes. The words echo tragedy, but the tune transcends tragedy, bringing resolution. Music and humor in the face of tragedy, then, become insights offered through *O Brother, Where Art Thou?*

Another aspect to this film is the very openness of our stories. The film builds upon a classic of ancient Greece, and a classic of film history. The story of Ulysses and his journey weaves around the story of Everett, Delmar, Pete, and Tommy, offering raucous moments. Likewise, the story of Sullivan and his travels is echoed in the adventures of these formerly chained prisoners who become friends. There is a constant play going on in *O Brother* between the source material and the creative imaginations of the Coens. In the process, it clearly appears that neither Homer's *Ulysses* nor *Sullivan's Travels* presents stories that are complete in themselves. Rather, it is as if each of these tales has an open conclusion, drawing to a close its own rendering of its own story, but at the same time reaching out for further completion by those who read the stories. The Coen brothers integrate both stories in a new telling that provides new insight. But if this is so, then they too are part of the same process. They have ended the story in terms of their own particular telling, but their ending is open-ended, inviting our own use of the story in our own continuous weaving of the narratives that make up our lives. Indeed, the ambiguity of an ending that is at the same time an invitation for yet another story is epitomized in Penny's haughty refusal of the wrong ring. Will she accept Everett anyhow? Will he have to go back to the lake and somehow scuba dive until he finds a truly bona fide ring that will satisfy her? We don't know. Nor should we know. The story isn't really closed—no story is. Every story's end invites a new beginning.

Despair

If the spree of violence can be ended through capture of the remaining villains in *Fargo*, and through humor in *O Brother*, the Coen brothers dismiss both forms of redemption in *No Country for Old Men*. This darkest of all their films takes us to new depths and new questions concerning the possibility of transforming or resolving the issues and problems that plague us.

We begin the story with a magnificent camera's-eye view of the Southwest: a desolate but beautiful landscape, shaped and contoured to meet the sky; gold of earth contrasted with deepest blue of sky. Its beauty calls to mind Camus's description of the "benign, indifferent universe" in his novel *The Stranger*, for the landscape simply is, just there, given in its beauty, an impervious stage for the fortunes—or, better, misfortunes—of its actors. In this superb beginning of the film, Sheriff Ed Tom Bell speaks about the atrocities going on "nowadays" (in 1980) as opposed to in earlier days, when presumably there was more human decency to go around. Evil is represented in the film by the psychopath Anton Chiguhr. He is implacable, remorseless, relentless human evil: the epitome of the evil strewn on the West Texas floor at the beginning of the film as dead bodies bespeak a drug deal gone terribly wrong. A young oil worker, Llewellyn Moss, has stumbled upon the scene while out hunting, has discovered a briefcase stuffed with drug money, and has run off with it. Sheriff Bell is the counterpart to *Fargo*'s Marge in that he is human decency—but in this film the evil cannot be stopped; decency can be overwhelmed. The sheriff retires (it is "no country for old men"), and the psychopath continues on his bloodstrewn way.

Toward the end of the film, Sheriff Bell drives out to his uncle's place in the middle of nowhere. Seeing Ed Tom's despair, the uncle tells him of a pitiless crime in 1905. Ed Tom has been depressed by the escalating intensity of violence, mayhem, and of greed for money so monstrous that human life is of no value whatsoever if it opposes gratification of that greed in any way. What might have begun as a simple greed for the good things of life has itself become transformed into something more than life—a cold and solitary rationality unto itself, belying even the existence of human community, in the single-minded pursuit of its will. To counter Ed Tom's despairing sense that something new has entered into the human project, his uncle suggests that it was always there—perhaps more under control, but there. We fool ourselves by pretending there was once, if not an Eden, at least something just a little bit east of Eden.

In *Fargo*, we saw an ending of sorts to the evil in the film as the one villain who is left standing is brought to justice. *No Country* denies this kind of an ending: the psychopath, having just killed Moss's innocent wife, Carla Jean, is driving away when a truck speeds through a red light, catching him in the intersection. He crawls, bloodied, from his car. Two kids on bicycles rush to him, marvel at the sight of a bone sticking out of his broken arm, and ask if they can help. Echoing an earlier scene where the bloodied Moss offers a passerby five hundred dollars for his coat, Chiguhr offers the boy money for his shirt. Tearing the shirt, he turns it into a sling for his arm, and he walks away. The boys then fight over the money, the act of kindness having turned into an occasion for greed. There is no neat ending here, no "bringing to justice" that ends the mayhem. Rather, Chiguhr is next seen returning the bag of money to the drug cartel, ready for his next job.

And what of the decency that redeemed evil in *Fargo*? There is decency indeed in *No Country*, first and foremost in Sheriff Bell. But by film's end, he is overwhelmed by his inability to bring any kind of resolution to the film's ills, and he resigns his office. There is decency in the longtime intimacy of his marriage; there is decency in Carla Jean's loving loyalty to her husband; there is decency in the "little folk" along the way in this film. There is decency in the heavyset woman who refuses to tell Chiguhr anything about Llewellyn Moss. Chiguhr spares her life only by the chance sound of a toilet flushing in the trailer, which would complicate her simple murder with the annoyance of another one. There is decency in the frightened and bewildered gas-station owner, who, confronted by Chiguhr's strange brand of rationality, escapes certain death. As in *Fargo*, so in *No Country*, there is decency to spare in the "little folk." But in *No Country* these decencies are engulfed in a vast web of greed and violence that acts out of no standard of communal good at all. The decencies of "little folk" are overwhelmed in evil, escaping it—if they do—only by chance. The decency that serves redemptively in *Fargo* becomes simply a witness to despair in *No Country for Old Men*.

And what of the humor and music that counters the violence in *O Brother*? There is humor aplenty in *No Country*, mostly mediated through the wry comments of Sheriff Bell. The humor catches us unawares; for example, we are absorbed as we accompany Sheriff Bell and his assistant to the desert floor. With them, we again take in the bloody scene of strewn bodies and bullets. The deputy says, "It's a mess, ain't it?" and the sheriff laconically replies, as only Tommy Lee Jones can, "If it ain't, it'll do until the real mess gets here." We are startled by the humor—not to laughter, as in *O Brother*, but to shock, that there can be humor at all in the grimness of the moment. The humor is not redemptive; it is a heartbreaking contrast to the evil it observes but cannot undo.

In *O Brother*, one of the answers to violence is beauty, specifically the beauty of music plaintively sung. In *No Country*, the beauty is visual rather than audible: the beauty of the land itself. But whereas the beauty of song in *O Brother* brings warmth to the tale, the beauty of the landscape in *No Country* brings only distance, majesty, and indifference. There is no comfort in this beauty, only awe.

So, then, is there any transformation of evil in *No Country*, or is its message simply a message of despair? Have the forces of evil, of violence, become too much for us? In a sense, as the response to evil so deeply violent as portrayed in *No Country*, despair may be the only option available. The film is set in 1980, with many a reference to the Vietnam War. But the film was made in 2007, in the midst of a new quagmire, the Iraq War. In 1980 we dealt with a cold war, with two nations aiming their nuclear warheads at each other—but two nations who shared more or less the same "rules of the game." The wars of 2007 dealt not only with a proliferation of nuclear weapons among sovereign states, but with the danger of nuclear weapons in the hands of terrorists and rogue states. In 1980, the issue of ecological destruction was but a drum distantly heard; in 2007 the beat of the drum grew ever louder. Is it the case that the Coen brothers made this film as a response to the intensification of evil rampant in the twenty-first century? If the world is barreling toward a destruction of human making, is it too late to stop? Have we become so insane in our greed, our antagonisms, our fanaticisms, that neither decency nor humor nor beauty is sufficient to restore our health? The evils that can undo the whole human project, and even the wonder of planet Earth as we know it, have become as implacable and as relentless as the Chiguhrs we have created.

Read thus, *No Country for Old Men* becomes more than a commentary on the dangers humankind has unleashed upon the world; it becomes a call to reassess where we are and who we are. The sheriff can deal with the problem by retiring; but if this is a metaphor for a response to human ill-doing, it is a metaphor to be resisted. To "retire" from the problem is to ensure that it will continue snowballing its way toward its—and our—end.

In a sense, *No Country for Old Men* functions a bit like the Ghost of Christmas Future in Charles Dickens's *A Christmas Carol*. If we retire—if we choose to focus on the small stories of our own lives, ignoring the runaway vastness of human greed and its spawn of ecological violence—then despair will indeed be the only remaining option as we hurtle toward sure destruction. The Coen brothers present us with forcing options in our confrontation with evil, both in our theological and in our practical responses. They force us to the question of whether human heedlessness means we have already foreclosed on any viable options that offer redress. Forcing the question, then, we are offered the path of despair, accepting that the monsters of our own creation are beyond our control. Yet there is the tantalizing path of a road more energetically taken—not a tragic humor ("it'll do until the mess gets here") but a comic humor, laughing with ourselves and at ourselves as we look for the irrepressible joy deep down in the heart of things, in the wondrous mysteries of existence itself. We will count on the decencies, foster the decencies, celebrate the decencies through intentional creations and expansions of communities of well-being.

Absurdity

No Country for Old Men is hardly the last word for such creative geniuses as the Coen brothers, who continue to spin visions and dream dreams in film after film. Two further films, the 2009 *A Serious Man* and the 2010 *True Grit,* offer alternative possibilities for responding to life's dilemmas. *A Serious Man* offers a way of sardonic absurdity, and *True Grit* explores two traditional theological themes: law and grace.

A Serious Man is roughly based on the biblical book of Job, which details the fortunes of a good man who has garnered many blessings in his life. Job and his whole community are content to assume that blessings naturally accrue to those who are righteous. Blessings follow from righteousness; evil follows from unrighteousness. But suddenly the blessings of Job's life are taken from him, one by one, until finally he is reduced to sackcloth and ashes. Three friends successively visit him, citing the accepted wisdom that righteousness yields the blessings of life, whereas misery clearly denotes that one has done evil. Job resists this reasoning, crying out to God to justify him. And God finally appears in a whirlwind. But the only answer to Job's plaint is not reasons, but revelations of the immensity and mystery of God and creation, dwarfing Job and his complaints into insignificance. Some scholars consider the voice from the whirlwind to be the conclusion of the book of Job, whereas others view the now final chapter, where Job receives double everything he has lost, as the appropriate ending. The problem with the added ending, of course, is that whereas the entire book challenges the notion that good or bad fortunes follow from good or bad deeds, the additional chapter reinstates this. In loosely basing *A Serious Man* on the book of Job, the Coen

Brothers choose to end their story with the whirlwind, and not with the "all's well that ends well" of Job's added chapter.

The book of Job adds one more complication: a prologue, set in the courts of heaven, where God is having an argument with Satan. In effect, Satan says that it is no wonder Job loves God and acts righteously, look at all the favors he has received! If it weren't for all this good fortune, Job would not be quite so righteous. God answers the challenge, giving Satan permission to tempt Job in any way he likes, save that Satan is not to kill Job. The story of Job's sorrows is thus explained, and the narrator goes on with the story.

The Coen brothers also begin *A Serious Man* with a prologue, set not in the courts of heaven, but in a Yiddish home in eastern Europe in another century on a snowy night. A man arrives home during a snowstorm, telling his wife how lucky he was to be helped in the midst of an accident by an old friend unexpectedly encountered. The wife responds that the man died three yeas ago; the so-called helper is undoubtedly a "dybbuk," an evil spirit come back from the dead.

"But I've invited him to dinner!" says the man, as the friend/spirit arrives.

The wife stabs the man to prove he is an evil spirit; blood seeps to the surface of the man's shirt, and he leaves, muttering that this is a strange way to reward a good deed. The question hangs in the air: aren't good deeds rewarded? How is it that the very good one does can nonetheless reap absurdity and misfortune? Abruptly, the film switches from the cold winter night and Yiddish dialogue with subtitles in English to Minnesota on a warm spring day.

We first meet Larry as he is undergoing a routine medical exam. He is a professor of physics at the local university and is currently up for tenure. He is married and a member of the Jewish community: his son is preparing for his bar mitzvah. Suddenly everything goes topsy-turvy in Larry's well-ordered life: his wife wants a divorce so that she can marry Sy, one of their friends and a colleague of Larry's at the university. Strange anonymous letters are being sent to the tenure review committee, suggesting that Larry is a man of questionable morals. Arthur, Larry's idiot savant brother, who lives with Larry and his family, is in trouble with the law. Larry's wife ousts both Larry and his brother from their home, sending them to live at the local motel. One by one, each of the ordered securities in Larry's life is inexplicably lost, and he is frantic in his attempts to understand what's happening to him, and why. Job had three comforters; Larry has three rabbis. Job's comforters simply offer Job conventional wisdom that has nothing to do with his case; Larry's rabbis follow in their footsteps.

Larry's troubles compound: a student leaves a large sum of money in an envelope on Larry's desk as a bribe to change a failing grade; Sy dies in an automobile accident, and Larry's wife expects Larry to pay for the funeral, which he does; Larry is tempted by a sultry neighbor. Nothing is as it should be in Larry's universe, and he flounders, struggling to understand why these things are happening to him. In the midst of all this, we are shown Larry in his classroom: he has just completed a proof involving a vast number of equations covering a very large blackboard. The proof demonstrates—with certainty—the uncertainty principle. Larry concludes the class session with the announcement that the students have a test coming up, and they should be quite certain of their answers.

The subplot in *A Serious Man* involves Danny, Larry's son, who is studying for his bar mitzvah. Danny owes twenty dollars to a fellow student for some marijuana, long since consumed, but the twenty-dollar bill Danny has brought to school to give to his classmate has been confiscated (along with the iPod in which it was hidden) by the rabbi teaching his class. Our young hero is in danger of a severe beating by his supplier, and throughout the film he runs to avoid him. At film's ending, the iPod along with the twenty dollars has been returned to Danny: Danny is just about to pay off his friend when the class is interrupted because of an approaching tornado. The students must all leave at once and go to the safety of a basement room. But once all are outside, the teacher fumbles unsuccessfully with the lock to the basement. Danny is about to pay his supplier the owed twenty dollars when he sees the massive tornado, quickly approaching. Danny is faced with the question, why pay back the money? Perhaps his supplier and friend will be swept away in the whirlwind!

Back at the university, Larry has just learned that he did in fact get tenure. But he also got a three-thousand-dollar bill from the lawyer he has been consulting. Larry looks at the bill, at the bribe money, and at the grade book, and then replaces the F with a C-. The telephone rings. The doctor who had been examining him at the beginning of the film asks Larry to come immediately to discuss something that has come up as a result of the x-rays. The film ends.

Like the biblical Job, the twenty-first-century Larry is given no rational explanation for the evils that have befallen him. He is left with the absurdity of life. There are no guarantees of happy endings. Job's encounter with the whirlwind gives Job some sense of a majesty and immensity beyond himself, some sense of a wonder to creation that dwarfs his own small concerns. The tornado about to descend upon Larry's world offers no revelation, only the erratic devastation about to engulf his town. There are no sureties, only uncertainties and a randomness of blind fortune. In this twenty-first-century version of Job's tale, the story is bereft of any religious rationale, or indeed, of any rationale at all.

The previous three films each contained a depiction of implacable evil: the kidnappers in *Fargo,* the marshal in *O Brother*, and Chiguhr in *No Country.* Serving as a counterpoint were the ordinary decencies of ordinary people. But *A Serious Man* replaces implacable evil with ordinary evil, tolerated and sometimes condoned by society. After all, Sy the villain is touted as "a serious man" in his eulogy. Yet he is a manipulative hypocrite easing our hapless hero out of his marriage, out of his home, and possibly out of his job, if his poison-penned letters to the tenure committee could have their intended effect. And if the implacable evil of the earlier films is missing, so is the rock-solid decency that opposes evil. Even Larry, who presents himself in his misery as "a serious man" worthy of notice and of help, fails in his final test: he succumbs to the bribe. The Coen brothers aren't giving us a great epic in this film, merely a tale of small lives in a small town with small goods and small evils, where the search for meaning in the midst of chaos is simply met by absurdity. The massive workings out of proofs and formulas only yield uncertainty. Absurdity is, absurdly enough, the rational answer to the random perversity of existence itself.

Resolution?

In the previous four films, the Coen brothers have played with four modes of dealing with life's ills: common human decency, humor, despair, and absurdity. In their 2010 film *True Grit*, they turn to a typical Protestant resolution of law and grace, testing the concepts through the vehicle of Charles Portis's novel of the same name. The film closely parallels the novel. The story is set in Arkansas and in the neighboring Choctaw country in the 1870s. What the Coen brothers do through film that cannot be done in the book itself is to lift up the religious imagery by weaving a hymn throughout the story. "Leaning on the Everlasting Arms" plays wordlessly as a constant refrain. Also, the Coens underscore the theme by taking a sentence uttered by Mattie Ross on page 40 of the book, using it as a voice-over at the outset of the film: "You must pay for everything in this world one way or another. There is nothing free except the Grace of God. You cannot earn that or deserve it." The inexorable law of "just desserts," consequences that follow naturally from actions, is contrasted with the interruption of this law by "good anyhow."

Tom Chaney has just shot, killed, and robbed fourteen-year-old Mattie Ross's father in Fort Smith, Arkansas, and then fled to the open country of the neighboring Choctaw nation. Mattie will see justice done: Tom Chaney must pay with his own life for the life he took. Mattie looks for a marshal with "true grit" to track Chaney down. She herself accompanies Marshal Rooster Cogburn to be sure he does what she pays him to do. LaBoeuf, a Texas Ranger who has been hunting down Tom Chaney for another crime, joins them as well, much to Mattie's consternation.

It is Mattie, of course, who has "true grit," proving herself in one situation after another. But after all, she has law (or at least "the right") on her side. She will see that Tom Chaney pays. Her small world is governed by law and order; she was her father's bookkeeper, keeping strict record of all accounts. And Lawyer Daggert is the family friend whom she often cites as ready to come to the aid of anyone she recommends. For Mattie, the world is structured around clear laws of cause and effect. Even the grace she mentions at the outset of the film conforms to the strict accounting of the Cumberland Presbyterian Church—although the mature Mattie, who narrates this tale of her youth, is careful to note that she found it necessary to transfer her membership to another Presbyterian church, since she eventually found the Cumberlands deficient in their understanding of election. She cites chapter and verse to prove her point. Law dominates Mattie's universe.

And grace? In the film's denouement, LeBoeuf has just saved Cogburn by a long shot. He and Mattie are watching Cogburn in the distance when Chaney comes up behind them, knocking LeBoeuf out. Mattie grabs the ranger's gun and shoots Chaney, who falls backward over the cliff. But in seeking to kill another, even in service to law, Mattie faces certain consequences. The rebound from the gun knocks her backward into a snake pit. In biblical iconography, the snake symbolizes sin and evil; to be bitten by the snake is to participate in evil and its consequent, death. And Mattie is bitten and trapped. With LeBoeuf unconscious, there is no one to rescue her: Mattie will die.

But Marshal Cogburn arrives and comes to her rescue, lowering himself into the pit to save her, cutting her hand to draw out what he can of the poison, then binding himself to her as the roused LaBoeuf draws them both up. Unless Mattie can get to a doctor, the snake poison will kill her. So the marshal, with Mattie in his arms, mounts Mattie's pony and begins the long hard race toward civilization and salvation. And here the background music of the hymn blends with the pounding of the pony's hooves as Mattie leans into the marshal's arms. The miles are long, and finally the pony falters and dies; the marshal picks Mattie up, taking the place of the pony, running with her in his arms until he too drops. But we see the light of a house in the darkness. The marshal fires an alarm shot, we see a person appear on the porch, and the scene fades. Mattie is saved: not by law but by leaning into the arms of grace.

There is a coda to the film, which takes place twenty-five years later. Mattie, now a stern and upright one-armed woman, is a banker. She has tried unsuccessfully to be in touch with Marshal Cogburn through the years, and finally she has received a notice from him that he will be appearing at Fort Smith in a traveling road show. Mattie travels to see him, arriving three days after his death in another town, where he has been unceremoniously buried. Mattie has the marshal's body disinterred and brought to her own town for reburial in her family plot. The film ends as we watch her standing by his gravestone, then walking away. Her voice-over tells us that time takes away all things. As the credits roll, we finally hear the words to the hymn as the Coen brothers give us the voice of Iris DeMent, plaintively singing "Leaning on the Everlasting Arms."

Five films, each portraying forms of evil within human existence, each giving an alternate way of dealing with evil. Evil is portrayed variously: as implacable in *Fargo*'s kidnappers, in *O Brother*'s marshal, and in *No Country*'s Chiguhr; as banal in *A Serious Man*; and rather traditionally in the western format of *True Grit*. Whereas the films of Eastwood, Allen, and Spike Lee can be read as following and developing a single trajectory of responses to evil, the Coen brothers offer alternative paths. Human decency, humor, despair, absurdity, and traditional values of law and grace all are tried, but they are not pitted against one other; one does not trump the others as the one-and-only answer. It is more as if we live in a universe where there are necessarily multiple modes of dealing with the harshness we experience. Evil itself is a hydra, a many-headed monster, and more than one resolution is required, depending upon the circumstances and resources available.

Despite the resources, there is never a complete resolution. If the book of Job, which serves as the paradigm for *A Serious*

Man, adds a final chapter that totally undoes the effects of evil, the Coen brothers know better than to take that route. The devastations of *Fargo* are not redressed; Everett in *O Brother* will not find the ring. Chiguhr continues his destructive ways in *No Country*. Larry changes the grade in *A Serious Man*, and Mattie loses her arm, though not her life, in *True Grit*. All resolutions are partial. Nonetheless, they are responses that reach deeper than the evil, touching a core that witnesses to the ephemeral beauty and marvel of life and goodness, despite the ambiguities, or even because of the ambiguities. And it is enough.

5

John Sayles

Corruptions

Matewan (1987)
Men with Guns (1997)
Silver City (2004)
Amigo (2010)

John Sayles confronts forms of social corruption in his films, exposing its devastating effects in the personal and civic fabric of society. He exposes the devastation of economic exploitation in coal-mining practices in West Virginia, the insanity of war as depicted in a Central American country, the chicanery in politics caused by webs of political and religious lies, and the immorality of colonialism in American history. All these forms of corruption are interrelated, and all call contemporary America into question.

Economic Corruption

The 1987 *Matewan* is based on actual events that occurred in 1920s Matewan, West Virginia, home of the historic Hatfield–McCoy feud. The film takes us into the plight of miners and their families through the exploitive practices of the Stone Mountain Coal Company. The mood is set from the first scene, prior to the roll of credits, in the darkness of the mine itself—blackened faces, somber walls of coal, and bleak lights streaming from the mining caps. Into this claustrophobic scene comes a messenger with the news that the mining company has retaliated against the miners' threat of unionization by decreasing the amount paid for each ton the miners bring out. The miners are paid, of course, not in cash, but in scrip, which can only be spent at the company store, or as rent for the company-owned houses—with the company raising costs all around, even as they decrease salaries. The practical effect is that the miners and their families are enslaved by the system.

When the miners nonetheless feebly attempt to form a union and strike, the company brings in Italian immigrants and Blacks from Alabama to replace them. But a "union man" named Joe Kenehan arrives, and persuades the immigrants, Blacks, and miners to join together to form a union and fight the company for better working conditions and wages. The company retaliates by sending two men who are essentially thugs to cow the miners into submission through threats and violence. The miners respond by retreating from company housing and land, establishing instead a tent city on the mountain.

One of the tensions in the film is the contrast between the miners' desire to respond to company violence with violence of their own and Joe Kenehan's nonviolent methods. As Kenehan repeatedly says, violence plays into the hands of the company because the company will use it to justify their own violence. But company violence has long preceded the actions of the thugs; it has been the violence of exploitation for the sake of profits. Safety measures, fair wages, working conditions, and health protection have all been sacrificed to the greed of the company. Interestingly, we see few if any actual officials of the company; they remain protected by the screen of the thugs who represent them. We are not shown their own pleasant lifestyles, purchased through the squalor imposed on the workers who produce the means of their luxuries. Their faces are masked by the thugs they send to insure their continued profits. Or rather, their own faces of privilege are masks, with the thugs uncovering their true nature.

The denouement comes in the Matewan Massacre, the final confrontation of now a dozen armed men from the company's agency and the miners, who have taken up sniping positions in the town's buildings. Here the film is chillingly faithful to history as company men, miners, and the union organizer, Joe Kenehan, are gunned down. The concluding voice-over tells of the eventual success of the union, and its capacity to wrest better (but hardly best) working conditions from the company.

An important moment in the film comes near its beginning. Joe Kenehan is staying at the boarding house of a miner's widow; her fifteen-year old son, Danny, is not only a miner, but also a budding preacher who preaches in both the "hardshell" missionary church and the "softshell" free will church in the town. We are given two contrasting sermons, the first from a fire-and-brimstone hardshell preacher, played by John Sayles himself. The preacher rails against Beelzebub, claiming that evil now appears among us as union organizers who are Reds, Communists, the Antichrist, and the antithesis of good. His fiery rhetoric equates the unions with Satan, sin, and everything evil. The very next sermon we hear is by young Danny, who preaches with equal passion on Jesus's parable of the Workers in the Vineyard from the Gospel of Matthew. In the parable, the workers in the vineyard are paid equal wages for their work, and generosity rules the working world. The film proceeds to play out both views: the company and its retaliatory practices are on the one side, whereas the union man and the miners are on the other.

The fiery preacher is apparently as poor as the miners. How is it that he uses his religious influence on the side of the rich, against his own interests as a poor man? A tactic of corruption, which will become even more apparent in *Silver City*, is to employ religious rhetoric to further corruption's cause. Those persons or practices that threaten one's luxuries are caricatured in negative metaphors drawn from the religious tradition, so that the fears and passions associated with those metaphors are transferred to the opposition. Insofar as the tactic succeeds, religion then reinforces oppression and exploitation; it becomes "the opiate of the people." The invidious aspect of the tactic is that its first step is the co-optation of the religious leaders of the poor, who then are manipulated so that they in turn will manipulate the poor against their own interests.

Danny offers the religious counterpoint by probing and proclaiming the texts from the point of view of the poor, seeking the core message of justice and liberation that is contained in the Gospels in order to empower the people toward their good. Thus both Danny and the visiting preacher use religion as social influence. The film puts the weight of authenticity on the young preacher, making the older preacher symbolic of an old order of entrenched economic exploitation. Danny gives a thoughtful interpretation of a text, whereas his opposite uses a ranting conflation of biblical images to condemn unions. But in actual practice the manipulation of religion toward social exploitation can be far more sophisticated than that. Is religion, then, along with its sacred texts, so very malleable? Insofar as religious people are kept biblically illiterate, the answer must be yes.

The one thread running through both the Hebrew Scriptures and the Gospels, as well as through many of the Epistles, is the insistence on economic justice. In the Hebrew texts, the litmus test of righteousness is drawn from Leviticus; it is the care demanded for "the widow, the orphan, and the stranger within your gates," a litany often repeated.[1] In the patriarchal society of Israel, such people had no privileged place within the social system. Whether or not the people were righteous was measured by how well the marginalized were treated. The prophets continued to apply the criterion; idolatry was associated as much with economic injustice as with the false gods whose worship entailed no justice. When Isaiah speaks of the nations streaming toward Jerusalem, it is not to convert them to Judaism, but to convert them to just modes

1. See, for example, Lev 19:9–18, 33–37; and Deut 24:19–22.

of life.[2] The Gospels continue the criterion. As Danny in our film proclaims, the parables that pointed to the kingdom of God were primarily parables of justice. When religious texts are used to further social ends, they can be deemed appropriate or inappropriate according to their fostering of justice, which maximizes the well-being of the poor by eliminating or transforming the structures that keep them poor.

If *Matewan* is itself a cry for economic justice and an exposé of corrupt practices, what of the resolution it presents? Realistically, the resolution is partial. Ideally, the resolution would seem to be nonviolent resistance to exploitation; Kenehan is a pacifist deeply influenced by the Moravians. The nonviolence he advocates requires a unity of the oppressed that embraces the differences that so often divide them. In the film, the "others" who are the "strangers within the gates" of Matewan are the Italian immigrants and the Alabaman Blacks brought in by the company to replace striking workers. Only insofar as both groups join with the miners, and only insofar as the miners are capable of overcoming their nativist and White prejudice, is that union possible. In the film, it almost succeeds. The canker that ruins its success is the infiltration of the union by a company man, who undercuts Kenehan's leadership and manipulates the men into taking up arms and forgoing Kenehan's tactic of nonviolence. The men's turn to violence results, of course, in the Matewan Massacre.

Is nonviolence impractical, then? Is it no more than an ideal? Sayles continues to explore the issue in his 2001 film, *Men with Guns*. Clearly, a title like *Men with Guns* suggests a film dominated by violence, and one might expect the gunfire to swell to wartime proportions in a film so named. But this is not the case. What the film unfolds for us is less the acts of violence and more the results of violence.

2. See Isa 2:1–4.

Corruption: Government and Insurrectionists

We are taken into a city in an unnamed Central American country, where the widowed Dr. Fuentes has come to the end of a distinguished medical career. As he reflects on his life's work, he takes deep satisfaction in what he calls his "legacy"—his initiative in training seven young people to become "barefoot doctors" in the mountain villages. Through these young people, he has extended the good of science beyond the medically insured city people to the poor in the farthest reaches of his country. But one day in the city's shopping district, he accidentally catches sight of one of these barefoot doctors. He chases him down to demand why he is not using his skills among the mountain poor, only to be told tauntingly to ask the other trainees why he is not with them.

And so we embark upon the journey as Dr. Fuentes takes up the challenge, driving into the mountains to seek answers to the troubling questions raised about the effectiveness of his legacy. In each mountain village that had been served by his doctors he encounters the devastation, not only of poverty, but of fear and both physical and spiritual destruction. Fuentes encounters the aftermath of the "men with guns"—and it made little difference whether the men with guns represented the government's army or the guerillas, for in both cases the results were the same: a violence that ripped into communal structures, shredding them to bloodied pieces. As for the barefoot doctors, each has been tortured and murdered by the men with guns. "Why?" asks the bewildered Dr. Fuentes. Who could harm a selfless young person whose purpose was to bring healing to those who hurt? The answer is that it was quite clear to the men with guns that no educated person would voluntarily live among the villagers unless that person was subversive, connected with the "other side," whether that "other side" be defined as the guerillas or the army. And so of course the barefoot doctors had to be destroyed by either the guerillas or the soldiers—by whoever got there first.

As we journey with Dr. Fuentes we meet a lone boy, orphaned by the conflict, who becomes Dr. Fuentes's guide. We then meet a renegade wounded soldier, who foists himself on the doctor and boy by force, always holding a gun against them. Our third journeyer is a priest who calls himself a ghost. He is haunted by his own refusal of death, which he knows resulted in the slaughter of the village he served. The men with guns had sent a command to his village. The villagers had the choice of killing seven persons—elders of the village, plus the priest—or facing total destruction by fire and gun. The elders convened the villagers, including the priest, and asked for a vote. In order to save the village, the elders voted their own deaths. The priest agreed, but in the intervening hour he stole away. The elders submitted to their deaths, but this was not enough for the men with guns: they destroyed the village. And so the priest was haunted.

The fourth person who joins Fuentes and company on the journey is a village woman who has been silent since her brutal rape several months past. She joins the doctor, soldier, and boy as they seek the final village—the Circle of Heaven—where the seventh barefoot doctor, a woman, might still live and work. (The priest has been taken away by soldiers and presumably murdered.) As these persons climb the final mountain, Dr. Fuentes experiences his own beginnings of heart failure. The travelers finally reach the village. Fuentes sits under a tree and mournfully soliloquizes about his lost legacy, his dream of leaving goodness in the world behind him. And like his dream, he dies. His medical bag, which he has kept religiously with him throughout his journey, sits uselessly on the forest floor. But a girl comes toward the now-dead doctor, commanding assistance for her injured mother. The soldier and the woman who had been raped stand quietly by, as the girl repeats her command: heal my mother. Silently, the woman picks up the doctor's bag and holds it out to the soldier. Nothing happens. She continues to hold out the bag, and finally the soldier puts down his gun, takes up the medical bag, and follows the girl.

Throughout the film, we are never given a reason why there should be men with guns at all. We, like the villagers, are given no insight into the justifying ideologies that promote such carnage. What we experience is the total irrationality of this wholesale destruction, which defies any justifying cause. We are not allowed to identify one side as good and the other as bad. Rather, soldiers and guerillas alike are simply men with guns.

What this film suggests in a world besieged daily with rhetoric justifying wholesale war is the insanity of the rhetoric itself when measured against its effects in reducing human beings into monstrous "men with guns" whose purpose is to destroy. We are grimly shown the irrelevance of rhetoric when measured against the well-being of communities of people. There is no glory in these killing fields, no righteousness, no justice—only devastation. We in America tend to be a pragmatic people, judging the value of a thing by its effects. What *Men with Guns* holds before us is the effect of policies that promote violence. Through what rhetoric do we justify actions that destroy communities? The film forces us to look at the results of our actions, and to judge our reasons accordingly.

But *Men with Guns* does much more than this. Because we are brought into the exploration of violence through the experience of Dr. Fuentes, we are forced, as he is, into the growing recognition of the role of his own willed ignorance throughout all of his professional life. The opening of the film has shown Dr. Fuentes treating a person high in military command; to the officer's expressed concern about his reputation, Dr. Fuentes simply laughs good-naturedly—how could the officer's reputation possibly suffer harm! Several times in the film Dr. Fuentes meets with government officials, assuming their justice and goodwill. He at first accepts their evasive answers to his questions concerning his barefoot doctors, but we experience with him the falling of scales from his eyes as he slowly accepts the enormity of governmental acts of violence. His loss of ignorance is at the same time his loss of presumed innocence. What he comes to recognize is that his moral blindness has in fact contributed to the violence, allowing it to be untrammeled by any efforts on his own part to challenge or stop it. The passivity of Dr. Fuentes and the many like him as they/we remain safely within constricted social roles is morally culpable.

Through his unjustifiable ignorance, Dr. Fuentes has participated in the destruction of his own legacy.

At this point we might be prone to seek refuge in our own American citizenship. After all, we are not members of Dr. Fuentes's society; we are not culpable in our ignorance of his country's devastation. But director Sayles has introduced two American tourists into the film who are in Central America to study Mayan ruins. While the country writhes in its present ruination, the American couple blithely focus on the ancient past, oblivious to the suffering all around them. We are those tourists, suggests Sayles. There is no innocence.

Is there resolution? Part of the power of any John Sayles film is its recognition of ambiguity. To go into the enormity of destruction wrought by men with guns defies any simple resolution short of radical changes in governmental policies relative to land usage, conservation, and justice. But to leave the revelation of the effects of violence with no answer short of these wide reversals of directions is to leave us with little but despair. Yet Sayles does not leave us with Dr. Fuentes's death and with it, the decimation of his dream. To the contrary, the film suggests at least two forms of resolution, two insights for our own dealing with the problem of "men with guns" in the world. The first is the moral responsibility of citizens to know the policies of their country relative to the well-being of those beyond as well as within its borders, and to act responsibly on that knowledge in nonviolent ways. The second is the hope that flickers even at the edges of destruction. Dr. Fuentes has not given the soldier who is with him on this journey anything like the classroom education that prepared the barefoot doctors. He has merely been a faithful witness to caring and compassion in the midst of devastation. The doctor has opened himself to the creation of a small community—the boy, the priest, the soldier, the woman—in the midst of communal destruction, and the new community is marked by compassion and caring. Dr. Fuentes and the little community that emerges in response to his compassion become the catalyst for the transformation of the soldier from being a man with a gun to being a man with a heart. We have seen the transformation beginning through the soldier's flashback confessions; we see it triumph when he accepts responsibility for the community's well-being in taking up the doctor's healing bag.

There is an open-endedness to the story. Is this act of transformation significant at all in the larger picture of society run amok? Will the soldier's transformation last? Or will the Americans wake up to the contemporary horror and ask the questions that lead to responsibility? We don't know. The film leaves us with an end that offers the hope of what might yet be.

Political Corruption

When we turn to the 2004 *Silver City*, that hope begins to disintegrate. Here the twin evils of greed and gullibility dominate as politics and profit succeed in an unholy alliance. Our hero is Danny O'Brien, a young optimist who saw his job as a reporter to include reporting the truth. For acting on this presumption, he was fired, and in the resulting turmoil lost his girlfriend; he is now alone. As the action starts in *Silver City*, he has found work as an investigator for a detective agency. He is given the assignment of warning three possible troublemakers in a political campaign that they are being watched.

The political campaign is a carefully managed affair, where Dickey Pilager, the inept son of a very canny Senator named Jud Pilager, has been chosen to run for governor of Colorado. The candidate is not evil, we are told, just a bit naïve and not too intelligent—his prime qualifications for office are his place in the Pilager dynasty (and they do indeed pillage the country), and his usefulness as a tool to undermine laws that interfere with the business empire of Mr. Benteen, covert partner of the candidate's father. He is "user-friendly," says the candidate's campaign manager.

In the process of carrying out his assignment, O'Brien learns the power of money. The Benteen organization utilizes undocumented workers from Mexico and Central America through an elaborate operation that, in an echo of *Matewan*, effectively enslaves the workers. The years since *Matewan*'s 1920s era have brought about labor laws that tend toward the protection of U.S. workers but not of workers who are in the country illegally. Through bribery and maneuvered changes in details of the immigration laws, illegal workers employed by the Benteen empire are ignored by the INS and are unable to bring formal legal complaints since these would bring about their deportation back into the poverty of their homelands. The working conditions are engineered to maximize profit rather than safety; deaths that occur are "managed." It is one such death that draws O'Brien into uncovering the extent of corruption connected with the Benteens and Pilagers.

One of the first duties of the new governor following his assured election will be to manage the release of public lands for private development by the Benteen interests. The land, says Mr. Benteen to our clueless Dickey, doesn't belong to "those bureaucrats in Washington" but to American citizens like himself, who can develop the land for private profit. He makes it clear that Dickey Pilager, when elected, is to change environmental protection regulations so that housing developments (including Silver City) can be built on lands left toxic by illegal mining practices—and, of course, to influence legislation so that the restrictions on toxic-waste disposal are softened. It is also mentioned that a "business-friendly" man will be put in charge of environmental protection.

Throughout *Silver City*, we are given the campaign slogans of Dickey Pilager. He is for "freedom," "the people," "education," "health care," "the family," and every catchword that will appeal to a gullible public. The gullibility of the public is fostered in that Benteen owns the media. News is faithful dissemination of the political message, interspersed with entertainment: reality shows, consumer advertising, talk shows, and conservative religious telecasts.

Money flows between Benteen and Senator Pilager. For example, Senator Pilager owns vast tracts of land; Benteen owns the mineral rights, purchased for enormous sums of money that fueled the Senator's political campaigns. Money also flows along all the lines of profit, buying influence in all sectors of society. Money, and the power it purchases, is the highest value, overriding anything and anyone standing in its path. Through money and for money, the Benteens and Pilagers stand above the law and morality with what seems tantamount to absolute power.

Silver City does nothing to suggest the possibility that this power can be successfully challenged or that O'Brien will finally win the day, and perhaps get his old reporting job back. Indeed, by the end of the film our enterprising Danny O'Brien has even lost his investigator job by being too curious about the business practices of the Benteens and Pilagers. The final shot shows the would-be (and probably will-be) governor giving a televised speech for "freedom and American values" by the shores of a beautiful mountain lake. While the speech drones on, the camera moves toward the surface of the lake, where first one, then several, then a multitude of dead fish surface from its toxic waters.

Silver City is a study of the violence entailed as the tentacles of corruption work through the political system to sicken every aspect of society. As in *Men with Guns*, so in *Silver City* the public is indicted for its somnolence. For all its status as fiction, the film invites parallels between the Pilager dynasty and the dynasties of American politics. The implication of such comparisons is that the very gullibility of the public is complicit in all political corruption. Even though the media (in its own corruption) conspire to deaden the public's sensitivity, whether through ultra-religious rhetoric or through waves of television violence, the public is ultimately responsible for its ignorance as it votes for the corrupting powers. Just as the Coen brothers' *No Country for Old Men* ends in despair, so also does John Sayles's *Silver City*. The corruption is so entrenched, so powerful, that it is portrayed as the way of things, as capable of smashing every obstacle in its path.

And yet the very making of *Silver City* betrays a hope. Could Americans but awaken, open their eyes, see the system so broken, would they not exchange their political gullibility for political responsibility, and overwhelmingly vote for a more just government? If the story of the Pilagers echoes the story of American politics, could the film itself illumine politics, incite change? Or—and here is the despair again—is it simply the case that greed gains the power to corrupt any regime, including the power to manipulate the public into supporting the very systems that undermine its good?

Silver City raises yet another issue. The gubernatorial candidate is a religious man, and at one point is shown meeting with a televangelist named Billy. The televangelist, no less than Mr. Benteen, wishes to use the candidate to foster his own agenda. Their interests coincide insofar as keeping religious voters focused on private sexual issues can deflect them from social and political concerns, blinding them to corruption. The film derides the televangelist; he is but a part of the wider web spun to render the electorate ineffective. Is there no proper role, then, for religious people to influence government?

Seeking political influence, and voting for those who favor one's point of view, is a privilege built into democracy; lobbying is a political right. The issue is not whether or not religious people or organizations seek influence, but the narrowness or breadth of well-being reflected in the influence sought. We belong to a pluralistic society, and by the constitution no single religion can serve as the established norm for others. Religions seeking influence must do so with the wider good of a pluralistic society in mind. Clearly, how that wider good is defined will be a matter of contest, requiring public debate among persons with opposing views and respectful openness to differences. These, in turn, must influence one's agenda in seeking to influence the body politic toward the common good.

Breadth of vision must include sensitivity to the proneness of the political process to corruption. In principle, elected officials are bound to temper regional interests with the widest common good. But as *Silver City* illustrates, elected officials are vulnerable to the interests of those who can contribute financially to the ever more costly process of getting elected at all. The additional temptation is to benefit personally as well as politically from bribery. Responsible participation in the political process, then, requires acknowledgment of the potential for corruption, and active support for checks and balances in the private and public sectors. A key component of retaining checks and balances is restoring investigative reporting in independent news media, and guaranteeing against monolithic ownership of the media; such monolithic news organizations are portrayed in *Silver City*, and are increasingly dominant in America.

With respect to redemption, *Silver City* suggests resolution by way of absence. Sayles portrays the situation as corrupt beyond redress, with religion colluding in the corruption. Danny O'Brien walks away with slumped shoulders, jobless. Again and again throughout the film, he has been told that he's a loser, and he himself believes it. The standards that pronounce him so are the standards of corruption. Resisting corruption, he is defined by a corrupt society as a loser. But we the viewers know differently—we have seen him prove his moral integrity and his own dignity. He has used his severance pay to ship the murdered immigrant's body back to his home for burial, and then sent the remainder of his money to the family of the slain man. Although we see him walking away with slumped shoulders, we also see that the woman he loves is again beside him, finally recognizing his worth. He is no loser.

Silver City is a passionate call for citizens to wake up to the political corruption that has overtaken us, and to use the power of the vote to address it. From both *Men with Guns* and *Silver City* we know that Sayles deplores the ignorance that fosters the status quo of corruption, whether that ignorance comes about through a populace lulled by media manipulation, or simply by the populace's being wrapped up in its private life and love and is heedless of wider issues. *Matewan* offered hope that through dedicated and sacrificial effort, "little people" could join together and effect social change. But by *Silver City*, that hope has shrunk to a bare glimmer, if it is there at all. We are left with Danny walking away with slumped shoulders.

Is this sufficient? Is it the case that it is no longer possible for persons to band together to fight against the corruption that undermines and destroys the well-being of both the city and the environment? Must *Matewan* give way to *Silver City*? The middle film, *Men with Guns*, offers a via media. There Sayles suggests that while exchanging one's ignorance for informed knowledge may lead one to the brink of despair, it is not necessary to fall beyond the brink into hopelessness. There can yet be a banding together of persons that influences them all to pick up the bag of healing, and continue working at the task of well-being.

Corruption: The Military/Industrial Complex

Sayles's 2010 film, *Amigo*, takes us one further step. In this film, the corruption is once again corporate, this time through the government and its military. Sayles positions the film in the Philippine-American war in the year 1900. America had gone to war with Spain, ostensibly to free the Americas from European colonialism. The United States claimed to be freeing Cuba from Spanish rule that had claimed the island for three centuries. When America won the war in 1898, it arranged to buy the Spanish colony of the Philippines for twenty million dollars. Meanwhile, the Filipinos, under a leader named Aguinaldo, had waged war against Spanish colonizers. The Philippines was declared an independent republic in 1898. Its government was established in 1899. But America, having purchased the Philippines, refused to recognize Filipino independence, and invaded the island militarily for the sake of the resources it could provide for American industry. The Filipino military action against Spain then turned against America. Sayles takes us into the occupation of one village during this American war of aggression against a newly declared sovereign state.

The conflict tears apart once-firm notions of loyalty. For the Filipino, is it better to retreat to the jungle and wage a guerrilla war against an overwhelmingly superior force or to stay with one's village, guarding it as best one can in the midst of enemy occupation? If one leaves, who is to protect the women, the children, and the elderly left behind? If one stays, is one then a collaborator for trying to preserve life in the face of occupation? For the Americans, how does one uphold the ideals of democracy and self-rule in the midst of invading another country in order to take over its land and resources? Do we attempt to democratize the people, "freeing" them to follow our own form of government, even as we colonize for the sake of free access to resources not our own? Or do we brutally repress the people, vaunting our power to control? The film explores the conflicts.

Sayles focuses on two people: the headman of the village, Rafael, and the Spanish priest in the village who understands English as well as Tagalog, and can thus interpret for the Americans. We are also introduced to the small group of soldiers—"men with guns," if you will—who remain in the village to maintain a garrison for the Americans. There is one other character, the American military officer who periodically comes into the village to enforce military discipline and justice, military style.

The Americans in charge of the village are relatively benign; it is they who think they are freeing the people for democracy. The major, however, wreaks periodic havoc since he alone seems to realize that they are waging a war of aggression. The ordinary soldiers speak about "winning hearts and minds"; the major orders crops to be destroyed. Meanwhile, Rafael's brother and teenage son are in the hills with the insurrectionists; they perform acts of sabotage, such as snipping the telegraph wires put in place by the Americans, interfering with material shipments as much as possible, and sniping. The major insists on waterboarding Rafael in order to make him tell where the insurrectionists are hiding, and then forces him to lead the American troops into the hills to fight the Filipinos. Rafael, of course, leads them instead to a place that he knows has been abandoned by the insurrectionists. They, hidden by the jungle growth, have been watching the movements, and as the troops march back to the village, they attack. Three soldiers and five insurrectionists are killed. The major decides that Rafael has betrayed them, and orders him hanged. Meanwhile, Aguinaldo has surrendered in Manila; an order goes out that amnesty should be granted to all. Even as the amnesty is being telegraphed to the village, Rafael's son climbs to the top of the tree holding the wire, and snips the wire. Thus the message of amnesty never reaches the camp, and Rafael is hanged.

Parallels between events in *Amigo* and twenty-first-century American military policy intentionally abound: both *Amigo* and contemporary life feature torture, occupation, insurgencies, democracy imposed on lands ill-suited to them, and internal as well as external conflicts. How do we handle conflicting values? If distance gives us the wisdom to denounce the American occupation of the Philippines, what do we say about current wars of aggression? How do we handle the moral conflict created when the nation's high-minded ideals contradict the nation's military and political practice? Sayles gives the alternatives: retreating to our personal lives (thus becoming morally culpable for colluding in our nation's policies) or of joining forces with others committed to consistency between our ideals and our actions. If we choose to join with others, Sayles suggests that we necessarily commit ourselves to transparency in government, and to the power of the vote to hold elected officials responsible and accountable for implementing national ideals in national action.

Resolution?

In all his films, John Sayles suggests that the forces aligned against us are massive. The yearning for justice and communities of well-being are dwarfed by the callous greed of the mining companies in *Matewan*, by the mania for guns and killing in *Men with Guns*, by the greed that fuels corporate/political and religious union and corruption in *Silver City*, and by the grim will to dominate militarily in order to exploit commercially in *Amigo*. Like Rafael, those seeking justice can be left hanging in the wind. Sayles also insists that ignoring the problems and retreating into private worlds of personal issues is a major part of the problem. Public issues *are* personal, affecting the health of the community and therefore the health of its inhabitants, and finally the health of the environing planet itself. Religions and religious people are a part of the whole, so that *Matewan*, *Men with Guns*, *Silver City*, and *Amigo* all ask religion to strip itself of its narrow vision and slip out of its posture as opiate of the people. All persons, religious or otherwise, are called to explore what is just in a pluralistic society.

Will we respond? Perhaps John Sayles would have us identify with a final scene in another of his films, one not considered here: the 1999 *Limbo*. A group has been stranded on an unpopulated island in Alaska; winter is approaching; they have no cold-weather gear. A plane appears overhead, circling to land. It will be either the criminals who are trying to kill them, or friends who have come to their rescue. Instead of finding out who arrives, we are left with the stranded group on the beach, watching the plane, tensely waiting to learn our fate. The film ends, and we are left—in limbo. In all four of the films we have considered, John Sayles has shown us our problems and has called for us to respond. We are that plane, circling, but are we enemies or friends? John Sayles waits.

6

Ang Lee

Beauty and the Beasts

The Ice Storm (1997)
Crouching Tiger, Hidden Dragon (2000)
Brokeback Mountain (2005)
The Life of Pi (2012)

THESE FILMS OF ANG Lee are love stories, albeit very atypical love stories. In each of these four films, love is both desired and denied, with the fourth film, *The Life of Pi,* stretching love beyond its usual erotic form. *Pi* gives us a love not only for life, but all forms of life—even for a Bengal tiger—and whether that love is reciprocated is a question indeed. Unlike most love stories, where obstacles are overcome and love triumphs, Lee's first three films give us precious little triumph. He probes the anguish of alienation where there should be love, touching on the social dimensions within which human loves are constructed. What are the negatives that keep us apart—and how is it that so many of them are of our own making? In *The Ice Storm*, Lee explores isolation in the midst of marriage; in *Crouching Tiger* he considers heterosexual loves prohibited by social custom; in *Brokeback Mountain*, it is homosexual loves, also prohibited by social custom. In the first and third of these films, he takes us into the negative repercussions of love's failure beyond the primary couples. The failures are quiet, masquerading as convention, but they rip apart the fabric of life to show the wounded flesh beneath its fabricated norms. Is there redemption? Perhaps that happens only in our final Ang Lee film, *The Life of Pi*—but only perhaps.

Marriage

Action in *The Ice Storm* switches between two couples—Elena and Ben, and Janey and Jim—and their pairs of teenage children—Elena and Ben's Paul and Wendy, and Janey and Jim's sons, Mikey and Sandy. Parents and children mirror and embroider upon each other's dysfunctions. The film, made in 1997, is set in the early '70s; the sexual revolution of the '60s has been ripped away from its hippy moorings into the affluent upper-middle classes. Lee frames the film in two ways. First, *The Ice Storm* begins and ends on a train in the wee hours of Saturday morning during Thanksgiving weekend: Elena and Ben's sixteen-year-old son, Paul, reads a comic book on his way home from his unsuccessful Friday-night date in Manhattan. Between these beginning and ending frames on a train, we are given the past week's disclosure of the hollow lives of two couples and their friends.

The second framing device is based on the comic book Paul is reading, and his voice-over commentary relates the quandaries of the comic-book superheroes to his own family. The voice-overs blend back and forth between scenes of his family during Thanksgiving week to Paul on the train. The more power the superheroes have, says Paul, the more harm they could do to each other without even knowing it—just like a family. The entire film illustrates this thesis.

Paul's parents, the affluent Elena and Ben, have been married for sixteen years. They have tried couples' counseling several times; their relationship is a routinized sharing of a house but not their lives. Ben is having an affair with next-door Janey, whose own marriage to Jim is no more intimate than Ben's. Sex is passionless, a diversion from the boredom of equally passionless marriages. Both couples have two adolescent children, and the illicit sexual relation between Ben and Janey is awkwardly mirrored in the advances of Ben's daughter, Wendy, toward both of Janey's sons.

The ice that functions as chief metaphor for the film begins in several early scenes. First Elena and then Ben take an ice tray from the refrigerator, cracking it open to release the frozen water. Then in two scenes we see first Elena and Ben, and then Janey and Jim, clumsily maneuvering frozen turkeys from their respective refrigerators in order to thaw them for Thanksgiving—but in both cases, they cannot handle the frozen birds, which fall to the floor. The culmination, of course, is the ice storm that wreaks its fury on Friday evening. Only after the critical event of Friday evening—the death of Mikey, Janey and Jim's son—is there a hint that a thaw of all this ice might be possible. On Saturday morning we see the sun starting to melt ice from a frozen tree.

The death of Mikey is critical. His parents, along with Wendy's parents, have gone to a wife-swapping "key party" on the night after Thanksgiving. Car keys are deposited in a bowl; by the party's end, all participants are suitably drunk. The women are to select at random a set of keys, and go home with the owner to his bed. While the parents are gone, Mikey and Wendy have been experimenting sexually, on their way to mimicking their parents by using sex to stimulate depressed lives. Mikey decides to go out during the ice storm; we see him teetering on a diving board over the emptied swimming pool where he and Wendy had rendezvoused. Then, as his parents participate in the key game, we see him joyously running through the beauty of the icy field, coming to the road. He watches in fascination as the ice-laden wires bend; a frozen branch snaps from a tree, falls on the wires and breaks them. The released wire leaps like an electric snake, crackling its lightning into the sky in arcs of beauty, then lands on the guardrail against which Mikey, down the road, is leaning, watching the splendor of the show. He crumples, and his dead body slides down the icy road.

While all this is happening, we hear the train-bound Paul, offscreen, reading words from his comic book: "slowly the alien glow dies, but with it dies the light of intelligence, to be replaced by darkness." It's not easy, Paul says, to keep from just wandering out of life. It's as if someone leaves the door open to the next world, and if you aren't paying attention you could just walk through it and then you die. As Paul's voice-over fades, Ben has recovered enough from his drunkenness to drive home, and sees Mikey's body on the road. Ben brings him to Jim and Janey's home, where Jim, Elena, Wendy, and Sandy are waiting.

Janey's husband, Jim, has been the least brittle character in the two marriages. He is bewildered by the iciness of his marriage, blaming his own ineptness. When he announces "I'm home!" to his sons as he returns from a business trip, he is hurt by their response that they didn't know he had been away. He had gone to the key party without really computing its impact. When he and Elena are the only ones left, he awkwardly explains his dilemma, suggesting instead that they go for a drive—in the ice storm! Sitting in the ice-clad car waiting for the defrost to work, Elena asks if the seats go back, and Jim impulsively, desperately, reaches for Elena for quick sexual release. Abashed by what he sees as his inappropriate aggression, he apologizes profusely. Meanwhile, Mikey dies. The film then takes us to the early morning hours on Saturday: Elena and Jim have driven to Jim's house, where Elena finds Wendy naked and in bed with Sandy. Ben arrives with Mikey's body in his arms. Jim, taking his son and laying him on a couch, bends over him, sobbing.

The film ends where it began—at the railway station, as Paul's train, delayed by the same electric failure that killed Mikey, now pulls into the station. Ben, Elena, and Wendy are there to greet him, exhausted from the experiences of the night. In the car, about to drive home, Ben looks at each member of his family and he too begins to sob, leaning on the steering wheel. The sun glistens off a frozen tree limb: thawing begins.

This film makes two covert references to the church. The first occurs when a long-haired pastor of an "unconventional church" (as he describes it) sees Elena at an outdoor book sale. He is out of place—a '60s-era hippy in a posthippy world, representing a church that doesn't know how to be itself. We later see him at the key party, telling Elena (who is surprised to see him at such a party) that sometimes the "shepherd needs to be with the sheep." When she responds indignantly, he abruptly takes his own keys, and leaves. The church he represents has no answer to the dilemmas of the film.

So what kind of resolution to evil can we see in this film? The characters in *The Ice Storm* all seem locked into their own individuality, failing miserably in any capacity for empathy beyond their small self-concerns. The couples in *The Ice Storm*, adolescent as well as adult, strive to change the endless boredom of their frozen relationships. But their actions simply change the characters in those relationships, not the relational dynamics. Their mechanical exchanges of partners exhibit no freedom and no sense of empathy (much less, consideration) for those affected by their actions.

The resolution, if any, is to reach for true relation in the giving and receiving of life—instead of an icy onesidedness—in recognition of the full relationality of existence. Jim becomes the key, first in his honest recognition of emptiness and alienation, and second as he touches the depth of his emotions in dealing with Mikey's death. Jim becomes the catalyst for Ben as well, but it is a sorry state of affairs if it takes a child's death to propel one to a fuller form of life. Whether or not transformation toward mutuality will actually occur remains but a possibility in *The Ice Storm*. The closing scene shows the early-morning sun shining on a frozen limb in promise, as icicles slowly melt. But ambiguity hangs around the edges of the film, and scant resources are given within the film to help its characters reach beyond and through the tragedy to feel the shining of that beneficent sun.

Forbidden Love

In *Crouching Tiger, Hidden Dragon*, Lee takes us in a different direction—awesomely enough, toward beauty. Here violence becomes its own resolution, transformed through the martial arts into a choreographed dance of dangerous grace. The climactic scene in the film is a sword dance high in the limbs of swaying bamboo trees. Man and woman thrust and parry, bend and lunge, moving together and yet apart in a dance that carries deep nuances of sexuality. But the context of this dance among the treetops, as in the other choreographed sword fights in the film, is ostensibly a will to kill. Lee has forced a chilling interplay of violence and sexuality under the stern control of beauty that refuses harm to either party.

This is a dangerous game Lee plays, for we are agonizingly aware of the horrors of violence connected with sexuality—a theme that will play out in *Brokeback Mountain*. Our impulse is to protest the artist's implied suggestion that a beauty that refuses harm can answer so complex a problem. Domestic violence often involves a rage that seeks so-called safe expression, hidden from the eyes of society, within the walls of one's own home, and there is surely no transmutation into beauty there. Those who are victimized lose the very safety that the violator exploits, for their own home becomes the place of capricious pain where violence hides crouching in every corner, ready to pounce and pummel. The intent to harm and even kill in domestic violence finds no protection in choreographed beauty. Is Ang Lee giving us, then, an ideal rather than an actual resolution? Is he suggesting that the impulse to violence *will* find expression, even in the most intimate of relationships, but that there is a power for transformation that can defang and declaw the tiger? Can impulses toward violence be choreographed away from their original forms into a dance of life, not death? If so, then the resolution to violence is not its own violent elimination but its transformation into life-giving beauty.

Nonetheless, both villain and hero die in this Asian adventure film. The moments of death follow two hours in which all the skills of the martial arts are combined with fantasy-laden leaps up walls, through air, over water. Violence and its opposite merge to create something new, just as do the strong yang and yin of the title. In the philosophy of yin and yang, both yin and yang have two forms. The weak form is static: yin remains yin; yang remains yang. Yin represents the dark, the moist, the earth, the female; yang represents the bright, the dry, the sky, the male. In weak form, yin is represented by a static broken line, and yang is a static unbroken line. Each remains what it is. But the strong forms of yin and yang require that each be transformed into the other. Here, the broken yin line contains a power so that the separate pieces of the broken, static line pulsate, move, and finally connect with one another, becoming the unbroken line of yang. The strong yang line also pulsates, pushing its ends further and further until the line snaps from the tension—and becomes yin. Even in the film's title, the word *crouching* is yin, whereas *tiger* is yang; *hidden* is yin, whereas *dragon* is yang. Combined, we have strong yin and yang ready to become their opposites, each becoming the other. This play within the title is mirrored in the film itself, where violence becomes its opposite in dance. While the sword is a paramount symbol in this film, forming a strong part of the plot, it is significant that the sword never kills. It is a crouching tiger, not a springing tiger; it is a hidden dragon, not a rampant dragon. Violence is controlled so that it becomes its opposite, and the transition occurs in and through beauty.

With regard to the two love stories in this film, both are denied their fulfillment. In some respects, this simply follows the Chinese genre it models, wherein the hero dies in the lover's arms. But in both love stories, the barriers to love are cultural rather than personal. Shu Lien was engaged to Mu Bai's brother, but after her fiancé died, and she and Mu Bai fell in love, they were prohibited by cultural morés from marrying. Shu Lien's marrying her fiancé's brother would have been construed as dishonoring her fallen fiancé. Meanwhile, Mu Bai adopts a life of martial arts and meditation under the tutelage of a master. His meditation takes him to terrifying depths of spiritual darkness, and he draws back.

In a highly restrained scene, he suggests that time and experience have changed the circumstances of the lovers, that now they may marry. But of course he dies at the hands of his nemesis before the marriage can take place.

In the second love story, there is likewise no resolution. The prohibition against this marriage stems from class differences between the lovers. But in a mirror of the first set of lovers, the woman, Jen, is also drawn to the martial arts; she is the protagonist in many of the martial-arts and dance scenes. And in our final magical scene, just when it seems that all obstacles to her love have been removed, she leaps over a wall and flies away into misty waters.

While it is the case that *Crouching Tiger, Hidden Dragon* shows personal enmities and hardships overcome through beauty, it is not the case that the social enmities that set up so many of the difficulties in the first place are likewise resolved. The film suggests that cultural mores have the power to prevail over the human desire to love beyond acceptable boundaries. Ang Lee pushes this theme further in *Brokeback Mountain*.

Forbidden Love Revisited

This is a haunting film of profound sadness. Gone are the possible answers of the earlier two films, gone are the traditional assumptions of the interplay of sexual relationships. *Brokeback Mountain* tells a love story that violated the social norms of its times, a love story broken by the mountain of social prejudice. It tells of a quiet prejudice that supports outbreaks of murderous violence, like a sleeping volcano that suddenly spews its fiery death into the sky and upon its surrounding earth.

Whereas raw violence was hidden under the veneer of ordinary life in *The Ice Storm*, in *Brokeback Mountain* the violence is not under the veneer of ordinary life, it is the very stuff of ordinary life. It is the effectiveness of social norms to dominate the way we structure our lives. The vehicle for exploring the theme is homosexual love.

Jack Twist and Ennis Del Mar are two down-and-out cowboys who pick up what work they can riding broncos in rodeos, working as ranch hands, and—in this case—spending a summer in Wyoming guarding a herd of sheep on Brokeback Mountain. The rugged beauty of the mountain towers over the men as they unexpectedly fall in love. But whereas the towering mountain is impervious to their love, the towering society around them forbids it.

A history of abandonment provides the background for this love story. Our major figure, Ennis Del Mar, was orphaned as a child when his parents were killed in a car crash. An older sibling cared for him until that sibling married, whereupon Ennis was sent to live with another sibling. When that sibling also married, there was no room for the teenager, so he was cast adrift. We learn this tale as Ennis tersely recounts it to Jack Twist around the campfire.

"Most words you've said in two weeks," comments Jack, to which Ennis responds, "Most words I've said in years." Ennis is a man who has taken his abandonment inside himself, drawing emotionally inward when there was nowhere outward to go. Rejected successively by those who were his caregivers, Ennis is now a man who belongs to no one, who reveals himself to no one. The lonely summer on the mountain with Jack catapults him out of himself into relation.

Yet Ennis is also a man who has made plans to marry. He is going to marry Alma in November, but he has apparently not shared his inner pain with her. With Jack, however, he has opened himself and found acceptance and understanding. Ennis is shocked by his own sexual response to Jack during a cold night on the mountain when he leaves the spent ashes of the fireside for the warmth of the tent—and Jack. They become lovers, and scenes of joy and freedom follow as they sport together in the first flowering of intimacy and love. Jack has the fanciful idea of asking Ennis to join him at his father's isolated place in Texas where they can build a cabin, live together, and help Jack's father run his ranch. Ennis refuses: he will pick up his life where he left it and marry Alma.

And so we are taken to the little Methodist church where they marry. Four years pass, and then Jack sends a postcard—he is coming by. Ennis waits nervously, and when Jack finally arrives Ennis runs down the stairs to greet him; they embrace, then passionately kiss, just as Alma comes to the door to greet Jack. She backs away, saying nothing as Ennis leaves her for a weekend of fishing with Jack. Nor does she confront him with her knowledge on the subsequent times when Jack reappears and the men return to Brokeback Mountain. Eventually Alma leaves Ennis, taking their two daughters with her.

Jack, meanwhile, also marries, and unlike Ennis, he escapes poverty, becoming a successful salesman in his father-in-law's farm-equipment business. Throughout his marriage, Jack continues to spend what time he can with Ennis, always asking Ennis to join him at his father's remote Texas ranch. Ennis always refuses; he has told Jack about his childhood experience of being taken by his father to see the corpse of a man who had lived quietly with another man and been brutally murdered—possibly by Ennis's own father—because of his homosexuality. Ennis will not go to live with Jack, even though he now lives alone in a ramshackle trailer outside his Wyoming town.

We follow the love story through twenty years, focusing on the sporadic trips, and on the parallel family relations of both men. Eventually Ennis hears of Jack's death. Jack had developed a relationship with another man in Texas, even while continuing his times with Ennis. And Jack had been brutally murdered, just like the old neighbor of Ennis's childhood. Ennis goes to Jack's parents to ask for Jack's ashes, that he might scatter them on Brokeback Mountain. His father tells him that Jack had planned to bring his Texas friend to his old home, to build a cabin where they could live together, helping out on the ranch. And so Ennis experiences a double abandonment once again: he has lost Jack through death, and he has also lost Jack to a man who had been willing to be with him openly. The story ends as Ennis's older daughter comes to his trailer, shyly telling her father that she is going to marry and asking him to come to the wedding. At first he says he must work. But then he goes to the refrigerator, brings out two drinks, toasts the engagement with his daughter, and agrees to go to the wedding. When his daughter leaves, Jack opens his shabby closet, and fingers two shirts hanging from the same hanger—shirts that he and Jack had worn that first summer on Brokeback Mountain.

The mood of this film is profound sorrow at the rippling effects of abandonment, in its various forms, on each of the characters. Ennis is abandoned by his parents, by his successive siblings, by his wife, and finally, by Jack. Ennis's wife, Alma, is abandoned by Ennis in two ways: first, through his inability to share his innermost reality with her and, second, through his infidelity. Ennis's daughters experience abandonment through the divorce of their parents and through the uncommunicative nature of their father. Ennis's older daughter adopts the same taciturn ways, and we witness her pain as she tries to connect with him but cannot say the words that will bridge the chasm of silence. And Jack is abandoned by Ennis in his refusal to live with him. These personal abandonments merely echo the larger abandonment by a society that will not allow the sexual expression of love between two men.

The social strictures against the men's love are as tacit as Ennis's own taciturn nature. There is no ballyhooing of what is or is not allowed: to the contrary, prohibitions against such love are simply so woven into the structure of society that there is no need to state them publicly. But the power of these quiet prohibitions is strong enough to sanction the two murders in the film: first of Ennis's childhood neighbor and then of Jack.

Brokeback Mountain gives us the problems of multiple forms of abandonment and its attendant isolation, and the difficulties of love outside the acceptable parameters of society. There is a sad tenuousness to every situation in the film, whether for the primary lovers or in their alternative relationships. Nowhere in the film do we get beyond abandonment. And the prejudices of society against the men's love are so formidable that they drive each man into an attempt at marriage that simply increases the devastation of abandonment. Within the film itself there is precious little resolution.

Consider *Brokeback Mountain*, however, in light of the themes hinted at in the previous two Ang Lee films considered here. In *Crouching Tiger*, beauty partially transfigures violence. In *The Ice Storm*, resolution involves moving beyond mechanical relationships toward a sense of empathy and mutuality. Is it not the case that Lee has applied both resolutions to the problems of abandonment, social prejudice, and lost love in *Brokeback Mountain*? The film itself is astonishingly beautiful, whether in the close-up shots of the faces, in the stunning scenery, or in the haunting music that accompanies the film. Even the final credits compel one to stay within its power, as Willie Nelson sings his lonesome song "He Was a Friend of Mine." Ang Lee has given us what was and to some extent still is a major problem in contemporary society and has bathed it in beauty anyhow. This alone, of course, is not sufficient.

In *The Ice Storm* we see further possibilities for resolution. This 1970s tale highlights the need to break through encapsulated roles toward true relations. In *Brokeback Mountain*, Lee tells a tale that begins in 1963 and concludes in the mid-'80s. Twenty-first-century Americans thankfully exist in a time of accelerating change as state after state legalizes same-sex marriage. *Brokeback Mountain* shows us where we have been and compellingly calls us to continue the changes that dignify and support deep love.

All three of the love stories end in irresolution. We do not know if the couples and families in *The Ice Storm* can continue to thaw. The lovers in *Crouching Tiger* die, as does Jack in *Brokeback Mountain*, leaving Ennis with one more failure. What of this fourth film Ang Lee gives us? This time he leaves chilly suburbia, the bamboo forests of China, and the mountains of the American west; this time he takes us first to India, and then to the vast reaches of the Pacific Ocean. But *The Life of Pi* is still a love story, embedded in herculean obstacles: still irresolute in its final resolution. For all of that, it becomes a redemptive end to this series of unconventional love stories.

Resolution?

Each of the stories Lee has told is based, not on his own writings, but on the writings of others, whether a playwright or a novelist. *Pi* is no different, based on the enormously popular *The Life of Pi*, by Yann Martel. Lee follows the novel relatively faithfully until the end, when he makes significant changes.

The novel and film begin in Pondicherry, India, where Pi's father runs a remarkable zoo. The young Pi has a strongly religious nature, based on his Hindu birth and culture. Hindu sensitivities see divinity in many forms, so it is not too strange a thing that Pi as a boy is strongly attracted to each religion he encounters. He becomes a Christian and a Muslim as well as a Hindu, seeing no conflict in the different formulations for God that each religion espouses. To Pi they are equally beautiful, equally valid, equally mysterious, and he zealously practices all three. Lee inserts a humorous addition to the story when he constructs a chance meeting of the priest, the imam, and the Hindu master with Pi and his mother. Each compliments the mother on the religiosity of the boy, and each is astounded and upset to discover that the promising young disciple belongs equally to all three teachers. Lee leaves the scene with the religious leaders arguing among themselves, each seeing the others as misled rivals. Young Pi continues to be devoted to God in many forms.

The major portion of the movie, of course, concerns the sinking of the ship at sea and the aftermath of the shipwreck. Pi's father has to sell the zoo. He had been in the process of moving his family and many of the animals to Canada, where he would have set up another zoo. There is a storm at night; Pi awakens at a loud noise, and thinking it is from the storm he gets up, going to the deck to experience the full force of the exciting storm at sea. But the ship is sinking fast. A lifeboat is suspended midway between the deck and the ocean, and the sailors (who speak no English), are pointing at it wildly. When they see Pi, they throw him down into the lifeboat; he bounces safely on the tarpaulin. A zebra also comes flying into the lifeboat, having escaped from the cages in the hold, but the animal breaks a leg in the fall. The impact breaks the ropes holding the boat. It plunges into the ocean. Later we discover that the reason the sailors themselves didn't get into the lifeboat was that a hyena had jumped into it, and was hiding under the tarpaulin. Prior to discovering this, Pi, thinking that only he and the zebra are on the boat, sees the zoo's 450-pound, three-year-old Bengal tiger, named Richard Parker, swimming toward the boat in the ocean. He calls to the tiger and manages to rescue it before he quite realizes what he is letting himself in for, at which point he leaps overboard himself. Moving shark fins in the water send him back to the boat; he reboards it, and the adventure proper begins.

Lee takes us through the first days on the lifeboat. A baboon has also come on board, rescued by Pi from a large raft of floating bananas, and so we live through the tensions of wounded zebra, voracious hyena, chiding baboon, and the seasick Richard Parker, who stays out of sight beneath the tarpaulin. The hyena kills both the zebra and baboon, and is eventually killed by Richard Parker: now there are just the two, the boy and the tiger, in the middle of the Pacific Ocean. The boy Pi, who, after all was raised in a zoo and has a good understanding of the ways of animals, manages to control Richard Parker to a degree—or at least to let him know who is the alpha animal on the boat. This takes place laboriously, with Pi spending much time on a raft he has contrived from the life buoy and life vests on board. The creatures survive because of the supplies on board, including desalinization materials to render ocean water drinkable, and through the fish and turtles Pi catches. We live with them through horrendous storms, parching sun, and emotional pitches high and low, which rival the pitch of the ocean waves through which they float. Pi's religious sensitivities are in full evidence. Jesus, Allah, and Krishna are all addressed, but not in pleas. Rather, they are like divine presences.

Pi and Richard Parker spend months on the boat. At the lowest point, when both are suffering from hunger, thirst, and the deprivations of their hard existence, a mysterious island appears, strangely made up of trees growing from an enormous concentration of algae. The island is dotted regularly with fresh water ponds and thousands of meerkats. Pi and Richard Parker gingerly step foot on the island, which is spongy, but supportive. The meerkats become food for Richard Parker, and the algae on the trees is edible, providing vegetation for Pi. Of course the ponds become an endless source of fresh water. Pi and Richard Parker grow in strength. At first they return to the boat each night for sleep, but eventually Pi makes himself a nest in the trees. Each evening the meerkats rush toward the trees, climbing them as fast as they can. Soon Pi discovers why: the island is carniverous, feeding after dark. During the night the pool waters turn to acid, as does the underfoot algae, and the island absorbs all life in the pools and on the surface. So Pi and Richard Parker take once again to their boat, now filled with meerkats for the tiger, algae for Pi, and as much fresh water as they can store for both.

The film and novel take us quickly over the next few months, to a beach in Mexico where the lifeboat has finally drifted. The severely weakened Pi and Richard Parker leave the boat, Pi to collapse on the beach, and Richard Parker to stagger, without a backward glance, toward the forest bordering the beach. After several hours Mexicans discover Pi and take him to a hospital for recovery.

Both the film and the novel versions of *The Life of Pi* begin with a novelist coming to the adult Pi, now living in Canada, to ask him about this story, said to be "a story to make you believe in God." Lee's film, unlike Yann Martel's novel, returns to Pi's home in Canada at the end. In the film, Pi's visitor shakes his head in wonder at the conclusion of Pi's story. The interviewer voices his incredulity at its strangeness: living for seven months on a lifeboat with a man-eating tiger? Finding a carniverous island in the middle of the Pacific Ocean, which no one has ever heard of?

When the interviewer expresses amazement bordering on disbelief, Pi asks if he prefers an alternative story: one where there are no animals on the lifeboat but simply a sailor with a broken leg who has fallen into the boat, a mean cook, Pi's mother, and Pi. The cook kills the sailor and proceeds to dry his skin for later food. He also kills Pi's mother, and eventually Pi manages to kill the cook before the cook can kill and eat him too.

"Do you prefer this story?" asks Pi. The interviewing novelist notes the similarities between zebra and the sailor, the baboon and the mother, and the hyena and the cook, and asks if Pi is represented by the tiger. The implication is that this latter version is the true story because it is more believable, but that the story of the tiger is better.

Yann Martel does not end his novel with Pi and the interviewing novelist in Canada. Rather, Martel concludes the story with the cargo ship's Japanese owners coming to visit Pi in the Mexican hospital to see if they can learn why the ship sank. The ship's owners listen to Pi's story with incredulity. They have never heard of such a thing—a tiger, a living island! Incredible! One of the Japanese ship owners mentions bonsai in the course of the exchange. Pi does not believe the ship owner. Really? A tree two feet tall that lives for three hundred years? Pi has never seen such a thing. It is not credible to him.

As the ship owners continue to protest, Pi asks if they would prefer his story if humans, not animals, were on the lifeboat. Pi names the cook, the sailor, and his mother. The novel, unlike the film, implies that the story of the tiger is the true one, but that if people cannot believe what they have never before seen or heard, perhaps they must reduce an amazing tale to a more acceptable account.

Redemption in this tale is more than survival through an extended ordeal. The spirituality that pervades the India period of the film continues throughout, but on the ocean the dividing lines of custom, ritual, and competition disappear. Indeed, the competition never exists for Pi, although it certainly did for his religious instructors. On the ocean there is simply the "other" of the animal world, the "other" of the endless sea, the "other" of the mysterious island, and the unseen "other" of the spirit. Each "other" is both dangerous and life-saving. Richard Parker's presence provides incentive for fishing and for survival. He is a companion—dangerous, but a companion nonetheless. Pi credits the tiger with saving his life. The ocean is certainly both death-threatening and life-giving. It could drown Pi or refuse him drinkable water, and its sharks could eat him. But the ocean also buoys the boat, provides fish for food, and demands activity on the part of Pi, all of which are necessary for his survival. The island appears when weakness threatens to overcome both Pi and Richard Parker; it is a life-giving reprieve, albeit temporary rather than permanent. To arrive there is life; to stay there is death. And so the island befriends our heroes by making it too dangerous to stay; they must go back to the ocean; they must seek their future in their own habitats. As for the spiritual world, that too is sustaining yet threatening. This is no tame Jesus, Allah, Krishna, or God, any more than the beauty of the lightning storm at sea is tame. Death and life both are embraced by Spirit, so that even while Jesus, Allah, Krishna, or God sustain Pi's spirit, there is no guarantee that Pi's life will be spared. Redemption in this film is not any single external thing but the capacity to see in all things the dual qualities of sustenance and danger.

Would this resolution add to the situations in *The Ice Storm, Crouching Tiger,* and *Brokeback Mountain?* It would certainly disrupt the complacency in *The Ice Storm.* In a sense, it is already present in *Crouching Tiger.* The complex interrelationship of yin and yang, where in strength each becomes its opposite, is a holding together at once of life and death. Yin loses itself in becoming yang, but lives as yang; yang loses itself in becoming yin, but lives as yin. One could view the theme in *Crouching Tiger* as a variation of the theme in *The Life of Pi.* As for *Brokeback Mountain,* Ennis is so locked into himself, impounded by society's forbidding and punishing values, that he sees only forms of death, not life, for himself. He cannot break free.

The Life of Pi adds one more life-giving value—that of gratitude. Gratitude pervades Pi's attitude throughout his struggles: gratitude for Richard Parker, gratitude for the gifts of the ocean, gratitude even for the island's pushing him away, gratitude for life. This gratitude is in itself redemptive in that it inspires both courage to endure, and a kind of freedom that goes beyond circumstances. Gratitude does not blind Pi to the dangers surrounding him; rather, gratitude gains its edge—its transcending value—precisely because it lives into the dangers toward life, even though surviving the dangers is never assured. The love story in *The Life of Pi* is a story of the love of life itself in gratitude for being itself, in all its strangeness, in all its challenges. It's enough, as novel and film tell us, to make you believe in God.

EPILOGUE

Terrence Malick and *Tree of Life* (2011)

In all the films we have been considering thus far, the problems of human existence have been focused in one way or another on ill-doing. Accidental and intentional murder, deceptions, greed, rape, gang violence, corporate and political corruption, racism, child molestation—the grim list goes on, like endless variations of an infinite theme. Like a knife, Terrence Malick's *Tree of Life* slices through the sufferings that we impose upon one another to expose the fundamental suffering of human fragility, finitude, and the inevitability of loss. He does this by interweaving the story of a rather typical American family in the 1950s and '60s with the atypical story of Job from the Hebrew Bible.

The film begins by juxtaposing two themes: the quest for God in the midst of suffering, and a stated contrast between nature and grace. Both themes are highlighted by voice-overs at the very beginning: a visual voice-over in the form of a stark quotation from the book of Job alone on the screen, representing the voice of God: "Where were you when I laid the foundations of the earth? Tell me, if you understand"; and an audible voice-over spoken by the mother. As we watch a lovely child playing in a meadow, the woman's voice tells us that nuns taught her there are two ways of being in the world. The way of grace is a way of long-suffering love that does not try to please itself. To follow the way of grace is to accept being slighted, forgotten, disliked, insulted, and injured. In contrast, the way of nature only wants to please itself and get others to please it as well. The way of nature lords it over others and finds reasons to be unhappy, even when all the world is shining around it, and love is shining through all things. No one who follows the way of grace, she says, ever comes to a bad end. But the book of Job and the film itself challenge her assumption and her stereotypes as well. Midway through *Tree of Life* a pastor preaches on Job 38:4, using it to tell parishioners that harm and ill fortune are as much a part of human existence as health and good fortune. We do not live in a world where good is always rewarded and evil always punished; rather, existence is the inextricable intertwining of both.

Following the introduction of the theme from Job and the nature/grace dichotomy, the film immediately plunges us into the pain of loss: the mother, alone in her house, answers the doorbell, receives a telegram announcing the death of her nineteen-year-old son, and writhes in the shock and pain of new grief. Calling her husband at work, she shares the news, and we move with them into the first days of mourning. The comforters come, and the usual words are spoken: "He's in God's hands now," to which the woman responds, "He was in God's hands the whole time, wasn't he?" A portion of Psalm 23 is quoted, and we hear the woman's whispered reproach to God: "What did you gain?" The father's grief takes the form of self-reproach as he recalls his unnecessary harshness in the child's boyhood. And then, inexplicably, we are taken to the home of Jack, the nineteen-year-old's two-years-older brother—not now as a young man of twenty-one, first receiving the news of his brother's death, but as a man in the middle of his years: a successful architect who builds lifeless cityscape buildings of glass and steel and who lives in a sterile home, devoid of color, with a wife from whom he is distant. He has been talking about his brother to his father on the phone, and he lights a blue votive candle—the only color in the home—in memory of his brother. From there Malick takes us into this man's boyhood, and the man/boy's own wrestlings with nature and grace as defined by the mother, along with his questions: Why? Why? Why?

Jack's questions blend with his mother's, and then Malick answers by turning to chapters 38 through 41 of Job. Malick imagines the voice of God, not in the biblical words of poetry, but in astonishing images from space and from earth, from the Hubble Space Telescope to extraordinary cinematography of earth's mysterious beauty. "Where were you when I created the foundations of the earth" becomes, at first, ethereal light, evoking the first instant of creation; then grows into a burst of unutterable splendor. Image after image pours onto the screen, color after color, shape after shape—sometimes recognizable as Orion's horsehead nebula, but mostly a pastiche of wonder: interstellar space. Job's "Where were you?" is translated into mystery and beauty in infinite combinations, finally zeroing in on earth itself and its gestation of life. The effect is to render earth small, dwarfed by infinite beauty, infinite majesty, and seemingly infinite time.

Malick then turns to earth's own history: belching volcanoes, spewing out the gases that will become the atmosphere that will enable life; ocean depths roiling and churning until the stuff we see becomes the rudiments of life and what will eventually become oceanic life, and then land life. Mighty forests spring up, and those beginnings of life in the ocean become the magnificent life of dinosaurs walking the earth.

We are seeing nature, and in this film, to see nature is to recall the woman's words: nature thinks only of itself, caring nothing for others. Her words are given the lie in the brief scene of two dinosaurs, one apparently helpless on the banks of a river, the other crossing the river, seeing the prone animal. The mobile dinosaur hesitates, approaches the other, and puts its foot on the other's head. We think it is crushing the other—but no, it is merely touching the other, and then it leaves. We see the first dinosaur lift its head, looking after the one who has touched it. Nature? Grace? The one self-aggrandizing, the other self-abnegating? Neither characteristic serves the scene; it is instead as if nature is simply the way of things, and that way includes kindness.

These scenes of creation move to the cataclysmic crash of a huge object from outer space into the waters of the Yucatan: life is destroyed; life begins again. The scene culminates now in human time, streaming ahead to our times, to the middle of the twentieth century. We see the birth first of Jack, and then of his two brothers. We hear the religious injunctions of baptism and, later, confirmation; we see the parents' pride in the children, and follow the children's journey into self-awareness. Discovery is imaged through long staircases at crucial junctures in the child Jack's life. Windows atop the staircases open onto new vistas of what it is to be human. At one time the staircase ends, not only in a window, but in an attic containing remnants of a past, openness to a future. Malick's communication is most often visual rather than audible, intimated rather than explained. This communication style is appropriate, given his use of the book of Job.

Periodically through Jack's childhood we hear his whispered words to God: "You spoke to me through her; you spoke with me from the sky"; "before I knew I loved you, I believed in you"; "when did you first touch my heart?" We hear the young boy's struggles toward his ideal of goodness: "help me not to get dogs into fights, to be thankful for everything I've got; help me not to tell lies . . ." These two forms of prayer, the one of intimate questioning, the other of conforming to morality, define the boy's growth.

Jack and his two brothers are swimming in the town pool when tragedy occurs: a playmate drowns. Jack's immediate question to God is, was he bad? The question is from Job and also from that spurious definition of grace: if we do good, will only good things happen? If bad things happen, is it because we were bad? The mother's easy equation concerning grace (that "no one who follows the way of grace ever comes to a bad end") is put to the question.

If grace doesn't work, is the father's way best, the way of nature? We have seen the father's tenderness at his sons' births give way to the harshness of what was stereotypically expected of fathers at that time. He is arbitrary, ungiving, authoritarian, to be feared rather than loved. His own story, however, has its own tragedy. He is gifted musically and dreamed of becoming a musician; instead, he became a company man in the world of business. His native creativity turns to creating patents that somehow never make him rich or famous; we see him defeated in a court case trying to protect one of his patents. For all his striving, he fails (or is only mediocre) in the world of nature as defined in his wife's dichotomy. His fall comes when he loses his job. He comes home a beaten man, and from his defeat, he owns a fuller humanity. He tells his son Jack, "I wanted to be loved because I was great, a big man . . . I'm nothing. Look at the glory around us, trees and birds . . . I lived in shame . . . I dishonored it all and didn't notice the glory. I'm a foolish man."

And then, "You know, Jack, all I ever wanted for you was to make you strong and grow up to be your own boss. Maybe I've been tough on you; I'm not proud of that." Jack has resented and even hated his father so much that at one point we saw him restrain himself against the temptation to loosen the jackhammer that held the car safely above his father who was working on the underbody of the family car. But he now responds to his father, "I'm as bad as you are. I'm more like you than her." And the father answers, "You boys are about all I've done in life; otherwise I've drawn zilch. You're all I have and all I want to have. My sweet boy."

This ends the long childhood, growing-up scenes, but it is enough to refute the false dichotomy between nature and grace, a dichotomy already undermined in the scene of the dinosaurs. If self-protection and self-aggrandizement are named "nature," and self-giving and kindness are called "grace," they are not opposites but simply different aspects of what it is to be human—or perhaps even more than that—simply different aspects of what it is to be finite, to exist, to live. The qualities are intertwined, not separate, with now one dominating, and now another, depending on circumstances and enculturation.

As for questioning God about the pains naturally attendant upon life, particularly when life involves losing the ones we love through death, the film ends by continuing the cosmic story of its beginning. Once again we see images of the cosmos, of earth; we are shown an exquisite diamond-ring solar eclipse, when the sun is almost completely covered by the shadow of the earth save for a slim surrounding ring of light and a radiant concentration of light bursting the bounds of shadow at one point on that ring. We see breathtaking beauty, glory, nature. And then Malick goes beyond the book of Job—or perhaps, rather than going beyond the book, he offers a dim echo of that ringing phrase in Job, "I know that my Redeemer lives . . . And though . . . worms destroy this body, yet in my flesh shall I see God."[1] Malick has Jack walk, as he did earlier in the film, amid the carvings, not of cityscape architecture, but of God's living architecture in sand and stone in the canyon lands of the Southwest. And then we see a doorway: not now another staircase leading to a window, but just a doorway in the midst of the landscape, inviting this middle-aged man to go through the door. The mother, young again, appears on the other side of the door, beckoning Jack to enter. As he does, the scene changes from desert to seashore, and on the seashore we make out many figures walking amid the near waves. We approach two figures: they are the lost brother, now as a child, and Jack as a child, and his whole family; and indeed, the entire beach is filled with a calm beauty, with people walking, apart but somehow together, sharing the space. The image is of new birth, of continuing evolution, of life beyond life. The music we have been hearing soars into a Kyrie and then an Exaudi: Lord, have mercy; Lord, we praise thee. And the film ends.

So what has Malick done in this amazing and unique film? If my task has been to trace redemption through successive films of a single director, I have not dealt with Malick's earlier films because in them, he is not particularly interested in forms of redemption. With writing and with camera he tells stories of complex human behavior in cinematographically stunning ways, but only in *Tree of Life* does he concern himself with placing human stories within their cosmic context and at the same time using that context redemptively. On the one hand, Malick relativizes our suffering by

1. Job 19:25–26 (KJV).

putting our small stories within the cosmic context. But on the other hand, he makes us part and parcel of that cosmic context. It is not something apart from us that we merely observe; it is a part of us and we are a part of it. Our small stories echo and contribute to the larger story, and that story is magnificent.

Terrence Malick has given us his own equivalent of Job's ringing declaration of resurrection in the otherwise inexplicable scene on the seashore. We are part of a story far greater than ourselves, but even our small selves matter within that story. Now we know in part—or, as the Apostle Paul would have it, "now we see through a glass, darkly."[2] But there is more to our stories than this life alone, and in life beyond life we shall participate knowingly in that larger story, that larger mystery. The whole, our placing within the cosmic story and our being embraced by that larger story on some analogous seashore, is Malick's redemptive answer to the sufferings and ill-doings of our lives.

Can this answer embrace the forms of redemption suggested by our other directors? The breadth of Malick's vision is such that any number of resolutions might be subsumed within it. Eastwood's answers involved a repudiation of violence as an answer to violence, and then the affirmation that self-sacrificial love, even to the degree of the loss of self, could answer the problem of violence. Insofar as Eastwood's self-sacrificial love takes place in flawed rather than traditionally noble characters, Frankie from *Million Dollar Baby* and Walt from *Gran Turino* are similar to the father in Malick's film. Malick might inform Eastwood that violence is a part of creation, not an antithesis to it, but he would seem to affirm Eastwood's condemnation of unnecessary violence, as well as Eastwood's sense that sometimes violence can be used redemptively.

Woody Allen's tentative resolutions of accepting one's place and time for what they are and what they can be stop short of Malick's grander vision of a vastly expanded context for all our places and times, but there is no inherent contradiction between Allen and Malick. Allen asks for affirmation of life in the here and now,

2. 1 Cor 13:12 (KJV).

regardless of any larger vision. He also suggests a pragmatic value to some sense of spirituality that includes affirmation of a God, but only insofar as this promotes the ability to affirm life. For Malick the wider universe embraces our small lives, perhaps with a kind of affirmation that enables our own responsive affirmation.

Spike Lee gives a far greater focus than does Malick to the importance of community in all our dealings with life's problems. While *Tree of Life* assumes community, community never takes the central role given to it by Lee. For Lee, the issues and problems faced by individuals are themselves in large part social in origin and social in resolution. Malick certainly assumes the community: it is, after all, the sermon in the church that leads to Malick's wider vision. But in Malick's ultimate scene on the beach, most of the persons there walk alone. The reunited family is the sole exception. The community is tangential to the action and vision of Malick's film.

Perhaps the Coen brothers fit most easily within Malick's world, despite the wide divergence of ways the Coens address the ills they depict. There is a kind of grandeur of nature in their darkest film, *No Country for Old Men*, that transcends the littered floor of human ill-deeds, mutely suggesting that the story of the wider universe can embrace even our Chighurs. And it is the Coens who also take up the story of Job, albeit with their own sardonic twist. Their adaptation of *True Grit* foreshadows Malick's ploy of initially opposing nature and grace, then conflating the qualities. Like Malick's woman at the start of *Tree of Life*, the Coens' Mattie begins *True Grit* by separating nature and grace, but in the end she is saved by their confluence.

What of John Sayles? Does Malick's cosmic story, with its affirmation of love, embrace his work? Sayles, like Spike Lee, has a much stronger focus on the community than is found in *Tree of Life*, along with a strenuous call to the community to address the problems that are always at least partially of our own making. In a sense, Sayles could object that placing our problems within the story of the universe as a whole, not only dwarfs our problems, but takes the sting out of them, enervating any call to address them.

Sayles pounds home the realty of multiple forms of corruption that flourish in human society and insists that we wake from our moral slumbers and, as Spike Lee would say, "do the right thing."

Ang Lee's *The Life of Pi* fits more comfortably within Malick's universal story. Surely the conflation of religions suggests a transcendent story to which they all point. That transcendence is brought home to earth in various cultural adaptations. *Brokeback Mountain*, on the other hand, is more akin to films of both Spike Lee and John Sayles in its reference to the troubling role of community. On the one hand, it is society that has created the strictures that so punish all who fall outside the parameters it draws. But on the other hand, to be pushed out of community is no salvation. The pain of isolation experienced inside the exclusive community is only intensified by withdrawal. Authentic redemption requires that the community itself be reformed, redressing its exclusions.

I suggested in the prologue that we gain theological insight through tracing redemption in film. While I have mused on comparisons and contrasts in these brief closing paragraphs, using Malick's comprehensive vision as a way of considering the others, the richest form of insight is less in the comparison among these directors and more in the intensity, clarity, and beauty each brings to his work. Each is a master of his craft, and each stands alone in the integrity of his work. We can gain insight from their labors, but the more valuable gain is the lesson that we need not confine theological thinking to the parameters of religion or its theological disciplines. The task of considering our human plight and possibilities for redress challenges us all, whatever our discipline. It is indeed a magnificent universe. Surely there is some glimmer of hope that as we continue to probe our problems, we might not only do the right thing, but by doing so might even contribute some small goodness to the magnificence in which we are embedded.

Filmography[1]

Allen, Woody

- *Annie Hall* (1977; written by Woody Allen and Marshall Brickman)
- *The Purple Rose of Cairo* (1985)
- *Hannah and Her Sisters* (1986)
- *Crimes and Misdemeanors* (1989)
- *Matchpoint* (2005)
- *You Will Meet a Tall Dark Stranger* (2010)
- *Midnight in Paris* (2011)

Coen, Joel, and Ethan Coen

- *Fargo* (1996)
- *O Brother, Where Art Thou?* (2000)
- *No Country for Old Men* (2007; screenplay by Joel and Ethan Coen, based on novel by Cormac MacCarthy)
- *A Serious Man* (2009)
- *True Grit* (2010; screenplay by Joel and Ethan Coen, based on novel by Charles Portis)

1. Unless otherwise noted, screenplays are written by the director/s.

Eastwood, Clint

- *Unforgiven* (1992; screenplay by David Webb Peoples)
- *Mystic River* (2002; screenplay by Brian Hegeland, based on the novel by Dennis Lehane)
- *Million Dollar Baby* (2004; screenplay by Paul Haggis; writer, F. X. Toole)
- *Gran Torino* (2009; screenplay by Nick Schenk; writer, Dave Johannson)
- *Hereafter* (2010; writer, Peter Morgan)

Lee, Ang

- *The Ice Storm* (1997; screenplay by James Schus; writer, Rick Moody)
- *Crouching Tiger, Hidden Dragon* (2000; screenplay by Hui-Ling Wang; writer, Du Lu Wang)
- *Brokeback Mountain* (2005; screenplay by Larry McCurty; writer, Annie Proulx
- *The Life of Pi* (2012; screenplay by David Mogen; writer, Yann Martel)

Lee, Spike

- *Do the Right Thing* (1989)
- *Malcolm X* (1992; screenplay by Spike Lee and Arnold Perl)
- *The 25th Hour* (2002; screenplay and writer, David Benioff)
- *Red Hook Summer* (2012)

Malick, Terrence

- *The Tree of Life* (2011)

Sayles, John

- *Matewan* (1987)
- *Men with Guns* (1997)
- *Silver City* (2004)
- *Amigo* (2010; based on Sayles' novel, *A Moment in the Sun*)

www.ingramcontent.com/pod-product-compliance
Lightning Source LLC
LaVergne TN
LVHW051008080826
845145LV00009B/2510

* 9 7 8 1 4 9 8 2 0 3 1 3 5 *